New Perspectives on Mazisi Kunene

Cissus World Press

Dike Okoro

2

Publisher's information/address:
Cissus World Press, PO Box 240865, Milwaukee, WI 53224.
www.Cissusworldpressbooks.com

First Published in the USA by Cissus World Press.

Cover Photo/Design: Dike Okoro
First Published 2015

ISBN 978-0-967951140

TABLE OF CONTENTS

Preface

New Perspectives on Mazisi Kunene shares with readers
an interview inspired by correspondence and prolonged
coversations on the telephone. The focus of this interview,
Mazisi Kunene, is arguably one of Africa's greatest poets.
Kunene's contributions to African literature as both scholar
and artist remains significant, given his commitment to
writing in his indigenous Zulu language and translating his
corpus into English. Ntongela Masilela, a close friend to
Kunene and scholar who has written extensively on Kunene
oeuvre, shares views that center primarily on Kunene's
importance in African literature, and his role and place in
South African literary and cultural revolution.

This book take different shifts, from the post-colonial to
the theoretical approaches that bring to the forefront the
foundational basis for Kunene's poetic ideology.
Additionally, it brings to the fore issues and arguments
shaped by historical and political movements linked to
Kunene's voluminous poetry and his colossal status.

In the compilation of this book a myriad of factors
influencing and shaping perceptions of Kunene's poetry,
style, and vision proved to be useful to our examination of
his role as a leading voice for his generation. As it stands,
this interview which is both provocative and penetrating, is
arguably the scholarly coverage of Kunene's work and his
philosophy as an artist. Equally of significance is the fact
that I attempt to comparatively situate Kunene's importance
to African and South African literature through questions I
formulated to meet the expected outcome of my research on
his work.

Mazisi Kunene has been described by Wole Soyinka,
Africa's first Nobel Prize for Literature laureate, as a great
poet renowned for his epic poetry. I hope this book will add

both value and inspiration to the ever thriving field of African studies that deals with contemporary African issues, for it uses Kunene's poems and his commitment to Africa's cultural revolution to make a case for significance as a poet and a scholar.

February 25, 2015
Dike Okoro, PhD
**Concordia University Wisconsin,
Mequon, USA**

New Perspectives on Mazisi Kunene (An interview with Ntongela Masilela*)

- Dike Okoro

Okoro: How might we situate Mazisi Kunene's work within the axis and analysis of post-colonial discourse? It seems, for me, that his poetry, when examined closely, rekindles the kind of hope for Pan Africanism that is inherent in the poetry of Aime Cesaire, Edward Kamau Braithwaite, Amiri Baraka, Kofi Awoonor, and Chinua Achebe. Do you have any comment to make regarding this?

Masilela: I do not think that Mazisi Kunene's voluminous works can be correctly examined within the purview of postcolonial discourse because the epistemological principles that inform his poetics situated historically in African cosmological systems fundamentally contradict those that inform the logic of postcolonial discourse. Post-colonial discourse undergirded by the logic of postmodernity denies the possibility of truth, objectivity, rationality, the distinction between fact and fiction, between objectivity and subjectivity. The logic of postcolonial discourse is governed by absolute relativism. Consequently, it does not

---

* September, October 2010. Ntongela Masilela, PhD (Los Angeles); Dike Okoro, PhD (Chicago).

recognize the distinction between context and text, even though it pretends to give cognizance to them. Postcolonial discourse, in a way emanating from deconstruction, sought to deny the logic of modernity which recognized the autonomy of these conceptual forms however interrelated or imbricated to each other they may be. I think Mazisi Kunene would have sided with the logic of modernity against the logic of postmodernity; therefore, he would have been fundamentally opposed postcolonial discourse if he had cared to give it recognition as such. Concerning this particular matter, I think Amiri Baraka, Kofi Awoonor, Chinua Achebe, Edward Kamau Braithwaite would have concurred with the position of Mazisi Kunene. Since Aimé Césaire, who passed away two years ago in April 2008, and Mazisi Kunene, who passed away two years earlier in August 2006, formed a mutually admiration society, they definitely concurred on this.

Where Mazisi Kunene differed with the logic of modernity was in the *understanding* of these conceptual structures, which he argued that of the West were predicated on their own metaphysics that were subsequently imposed on African history, while his own were directly drawn from *African cosmology*. For him, this differentiation is inherent in the linguistic systems of representation, in very broad terms of African languages versus European languages. This is why he was unyielding in his belief that African literature should be written in the African languages and not in the European languages.

Perhaps the most intractable fault line in South African literary history in the twentieth century was between those African writers who wrote in the African languages (in *isi*Xhosa, in *isi*Zulu, in Sesotho, and so on) and those who wrote in the European languages (invariably in English). This historical divide emerged as a major intellectual debate in my country in the 1930s between two outstanding members of the Zulu Intellectuals of the 1940s, Benedict Wallet Vilakazi, poet, scholar and novelist, who wrote in isiZulu, and H. I. E. Dhlomo, poet, playwright, journalist and intellectual historian, who wrote in English. One can trace its genealogy among the Xhosa Intellectuals of the 1880s, in the disagreement between Elijah Makiwane and Pambani Jeremiah Mzimba about the role of the English language and English literary culture from Shakespeare and Francis Bacon to William Wordsworth in the making of modernity in Africa, particularly in South Africa. Given what has happened in the second half of twentieth century of South African literary history, Dhlomo seems to have defeated Vilakazi. Mazisi Kunene's intellectual hatred of Dhlomo, who was himself the youngest member of the Zulu Intellectuals of the 1940s, should be understood in the context of this intellectual duel. Mazisi Kunene's voluminous poetry, practically all of it written in exile, was, among other things, an attempt to overturn this seemingly incontrovertible fact of South African literary history. Having seen his many, many epics and anthologies written in *isi*Zulu and still in manuscript form, all in the city of Durban in South Africa, I have no doubt that on their publication and dissemination throughout Africa in translations, Mazisi Kunene will succeed in overturning this seeming verdict of history. Mazisi Kunene is going to have many surprises for Africa. Given all this, it is not clear to me what postcolonial discourse can do to clarify and illuminate these complex and complicated matters that were unleashed by Western modernity's violent entrance into African history.

It seems to me that Mazisi Kunene's unsurpassable poetic act was a desperate and dramatic attempt to resurrect African cosmology in the modern African world. This was absolutely daring. But is such a monumental effort achievable given that Western modernity has torn Africa asunder in every conceivable way? While he appears to us today as a great poet of African spiritual crisis, he may appear to posterity as the last great diviner of African cosmology. Let me add here that there are fascinating affinities between Mazisi Kunene and the great *isangoma* (medicine man and spiritual healer), the spinner of incredible tales whose logic is beyond comprehension, Credo Mutwa, who was also a member of the Zulu Intellectuals of the 1940s. Let me say in parenthesis that Mazisi Kunene has written a major essay on African cosmology that I intend to publish soon in an anthology of his critical writings.

I think Mazisi Kunene attempted to reach out to the black world, especially to the African Diaspora (United States, the Caribbean, and Latin America), through the principles of *African cosmology* rather than by means of *black cultural politics* which he believed had been tainted if not poisoned by Western capitalism, imperialism and colonialism. It is principally this preoccupation with African cosmology that made large tracts of his poetry to concern themselves with the dialectic between History and Nature. He would have preferred the word *interaction* rather than *dialectical*. This major theme is dazzlingly formulated in his anthology *The Ancestors & the Sacred Mountain* (1982).

The mutual admiration for each other between Aimé Cesairé and Mazisi Kunene was that they gave each other what the other was searching for or confirmed what the other had been hypothesizing. I would argue that perhaps the reason Mazisi Kunene was buoyed in writing the "Introduction" to John Berger and Anna Bostock's translation of Aimé Cesairé *Return To My Native Land* (1969) was that on encountering this *modern epic* it confirmed to him that it was still possible to write in this generic form which he had inherited from the great Zulu nineteenth century poets, Magolwane and Mshomgweni. When Mazisi Kunene published in exile what appeared to have been his first book of poems, *Zulu Poems* (1970) a year later, he published in it a seven-page extract of a poem called "*Anthem of Decades* (Extract from an epic)", taken from a manuscript which a decade later was published as a 315-page epic known as *Anthem of the*

Decades (1981). In the opposite direction, when Aimé Cesairé was composing *Return To My Native Land* in the mid 1930s under the aegis of Surrealist edicts and at the same time inventing Negritude with Leopold Sedar Senghor and Léon Damas in order to break with the hegemony of Surrealism paradoxically through Surrealism itself, Cesairé was searching for an African philosophical system; hence his admiration for Frobenius, which would anchor him away from what he was not trying to escape from: Europeanism. Senghor was not in a position to introduce Cesairé to African religious philosophies because by rejecting African languages in preference for the French language, he had unknowingly and, perhaps unintentionally, decamped himself from African cosmological systems. It seems to me that Cesairé was always searching for African cosmological systems, which he took to be the quintessential essence of Africanness, directly from us Africans and not from Europeans, which he accepted now and then from Europeans through default.

I would postulate that it was when he encountered the epic vision of Mazisi Kunene that he felt he had at last encountered or imbibed African philosophies or cosmologies from the source itself. This postulation is supported by the remarkable words Césaire uttered to describe Mazisi Kunene within a year or two before the African poet permanently departed: "The heritage of Kunene, this great spokesman is without a doubt indispensable to the restructuring of the foundation of the reconstruction of the identity of the African continent" (found in *Mazisi Raymond Fakazi Mngoni Kunene*, a deluxe hardcover booklet of tributes produced by the Mazisi Kunene Foundation on the occasion the great poet was ennobled South African National Poet Laureate by the nation on March 5, 2005). This is the most extraordinary praise that Mazisi Kunene has received from anyone! What can we mortals say after these words!

In tribute to the memory of both Aimé Césaire and Mazisi

Kunene, I would like to quote this short poem which appears in
The Ancestors & the Sacred Mountain:

Unfinished Epic

For the truth must outlast the prophet

And those who follow must bow down to this moment,

Choosing a place where to praise his mind.

Yet words are thieves that lull the watchman,

They seize the resting place of eternal truths,

They take the garden for the violent seed.

We are deceived by them and through them

We imagine a greater poet than was ever born.

Yet we must curse you for the unfinished journey.

Because of you a team of vultures threatens us.

Had you, by your wisdom, narrated the whole tale

Our children's children would have been spared the
humiliation.

Very few poets are celebrated in the country of their birth
as national treasures during their lifetime. How would you
evaluate and interpret Mazisi Kunene's appointment as
South Africa's first poet laureate by President Thabo Mbeki?
What is the significance of such an appointment?

I would not agree with your general statement that very few
poets are honoured as national treasures in the country of their
birth during their lifetimes. I could mention a number of European

poets in the nineteenth century who were recognized as such: Walt Whitman in United States, by a no lesser person than Emerson; Sandor Petofi in Hungary when the country was under oppression by the Austro-Hungarian Empire; Alexander Pushkin was also given cognizance which was affirmed by Dostoeyevsky later in the century; Alexander Mickiewicz in Poland when in actuality the country did not really exist in that century since it was divided between Prussia, Russia and the Austro-Hungarian Empire; and so on. This was easily doable in the nineteenth century in Europe for two fundamental reasons I think: one is that that century was a moment of emergent *nationalisms* against foreign domination; the other is that even for countries that were dominated, they never lost or abandoned a sense of *historical continuity* at the level of national consciousness or by means of their singular national languages. In Latin America too, especially during the nineteenth century, giving recognition to a country's outstanding poets was a badge of honor: Jose Marti in Cuba and Ruben Dario in Nicaragua. The Cuban Revolution in the 1960s honoured the mulatto Cuban poet Nicolás Guillén as a National Poet.

I think it has largely been in Africa that the immediate recognition of our outstanding poets as national treasures has been difficult to achieve. This is fundamentally because when European history colonized and occupied African history it ruptured too many things: emotional, metaphysical, cultural and so on. Therefore many of us in Africa have never had a sense of historical continuity and a strong nationalism because the opportunity to unify the nation with a new sense of national sensibility has been complicated and intractable. Perhaps much more importantly, our linguistic structures were severed from our metaphysical beliefs. Equally damaging, resurgent tribalism(s) have pulverized our national consciousness. I think the reason for Nigeria's inability to recognize Christopher Okigbo as a National Poet is that he participated in the Civil War as an active combatant on the side of Biafra and died in it at a young age of thirty-six years. Senghor's lack of recognition in Senegal is that he has been perceived as too French, perhaps too conservative in a strange way, but perhaps crucially, he was a non-Muslim in a predominantly Muslim society.

Your proposition is very intriguing and challenging because one could write a fascinating study examining the literary map of Africa as to which countries have given major recognitions to their outstanding poets. What about Jacques Rabemananjara in Madagascar? How about Edouard Maunick in Mauritius? What of Tichaya U'Tamsi in Congo-Brazzaville? The tabulation of obstacles to such recognition would be very intriguing and equally depressing!

The instance of South Africa is complicated in its own particular way as in any other African country. If one is to understand the real significance of the appointment of Mazisi Kunene as a National Poet Laureate in 2005 by the African National Congress (ANC) government, it is crucial to understand the political and cultural background of the two individuals who made this possible: President Thabo Mbeki and the then Minister of Culture Z. Pallo Jordan. They are children of the Xhosa intellectual aristocracy within the New African Movement in that their parents occupied prominent positions in this intellectual and cultural movement of the first half of the twentieth century in South Africa. Thabo Mbeki's father, Govan Mbeki, and Pallo Jordan's father, A. C. Jordan, belonged to the 'Magnificent Generation of the 1930s' constellation within the New African Movement. Both fathers were members of the Marxist wing of the Movement, though belonging to different ideological camps: Govan Mbeki belonged to the South African Communist Party and African National Congress; A. C. Jordan was a member of the Non-European Unity Movement (NEUM), a South African version of Trotskyism. Though politically and ideologically at loggerheads with each other, both of them were profoundly influenced by the great cultural revolution that the great Xhosa poet S. E. K. Mqhayi had effect throughout South Africa with his Xhosa poetry which appeared in various newspapers such as *Izwi Labantu* (The Voice of the People), *Imvo Zabantsundu* (African Opinion), *Umteteli wa Bantu* (The Mouthpiece of the People) and *The Bantu World* in the last decade of the nineteenth century and in the first three decades of the twentieth century. Let me add that Pallo Jordan's mother too, Phyllis Ntantala, was a prominent member of the New African Movement in her own right, espousing feminism and Marxism within it, and author of a very instructive autobiography, *A Life's Mosaic* (1993). In the preface to the 2009 edition of the autobiography she writes: "Like Trotsky, I did not leave home without the proverbial one-and-six in my pocket. I came from a family of landed gentry in the Transkei".

Because of the consciousness they had of the cultural revolution that Mqhayi had realized, both these New African intellectuals gave preeminence to the Xhosa language (African language), albeit from different directions. A. C. Jordan's connection to the great poet was direct in that not only had he written the best Xhosa novel *Ingqumbo Yeminyanya* (1940, The Wrath of the Ancestral Spirits) which is a direct descendant of Mqhayi's novella *Ityala lama Wele* (1914, The Case of Twins), he also wrote a remarkable obituary essay when the great poet died in 1945. Govan Mbeki, on the other hand, came to have a greater appreciation of Mqhayi's articulation of the language by hearing daily the speech patterns of the Xhosa peasantry among whom he was politically organizing on behalf of the ANC. Years late, Mbeki was to write *South Africa: The Peasants Revolt* (1964), conveying in graphic terms the oppression the peasantry suffered under colonial modernity.

Many other New African intellectuals within the New African Movement other than Govan Mbeki and A. C. Jordan also appreciated the extraordinary poetry of Mqhayi. Two other intellectuals preceding Govan Mbeki and A. C. Jordan could be mentioned here: D. D. T. Jabavu and R. V. Selope Thema. Both of these later showed their appreciation of the poetic imagination of Mqhayi in a direct manner: D. D. T. Jabavu encouraged his younger brother Alexander Macaulay Jabavu who was editor of *Imvo Zabantsundu* newspaper in the 1920s to publish many poems of Mqhayi; likewise R. V. Selope Thema, when he was editor of *The Bantu World* newspaper, supported Mqhayi's last productive period of the 1930s by publishing reams and reams of his poetry and prose pieces on a weekly basis. Observing the astonishing productivity of the poet in the 1920s and in the 1930s, D. D. T. Jabavu invented the sobriquet of *"Imbongi Yesizwe Jekelele"* (literal translation: Poet of the Whole Nation, or Poet Laureate) to characterize Mqhayi; a characterization that was endorsed through acclamation by practically all the New African members of the New African Movement.

Mazisi Kunene was very much conscious that he was an exponent of a literary tradition invented or founded by Mqhayi: that is of African Literature in the African Languages. Kunene's immediate master, his Zulu compatriot Benedict Wallet Vilakazi, was also a member of this literary and culturally privileged circle of enlightened modernizers. Mazisi Kunene became the greatest exponent of this literary tradition in whole of Africa across the twentieth-century. In the Introduction to *Zulu Poems* (1970), this is what Mazisi Kunene had to say of Mqhayi:

"Other African peoples of southern Africa show equal merit in their poetry according to the period of their history and national expression. For instance, Xhosa poetry has a rich tradition which was revived in more recent times by the great Xhosa poet, Mqhayi."

Clearly, President Thabo Mbeki and Minister of Culture Pallo

Jordan were aware not only of the connection between S. E. K. Mqhayi and Mazisi Kunene within a larger circle of *imbongi* (poets) in South Africa who wrote in the African languages, which would include, among others, J. J. R. Jolobe, Nontsizi Mgqwetho, S. E. Ntsane, Emman Made, David Livingstone Phukamile Yali-Manasi, Benedict Wallet Vilakazi, S. Dlamini, but also of his genealogy within African culture at large. For instance, in a Statement on the African Renaissance of August 13, 1998, then still Deputy President to Nelson Mandela, Thabo Mbeki had this to say:

> In that journey of self-discovery and the restoration of our own self-esteem, without which we would never become combatants for the African Renaissance, we must retune our ears to the music of Zao and Franco of the Congos and the poetry of Mazisi Kunene of South Africa and refocus oue eyes to behold the paintings of Makangatane of Mozambique and the sculptures of Dumile Feni of South Africa. (in *Mazisi Raymond Fakazi Mngoni Kunene*).

Pallo Jordan had this to say:

> Theirs was a generation that was in one sense extremely fortunate. Their good fortune was that they completed their high school education in the mid-1950s. They were consequently always a few steps ahead of the juggernaut of Bantu Education, which was introduced in African primary schools in 1955, extended to high schools in 1956 then imposed on universities and colleges in 1960 . . .
>
> After completing a Master's Degree in African Studies at the then University of Natal, Mazisi Raymond Kunene went into exile as an activist of the African National Congress. Under the leadership of that great African patriot, Oliver Tambo, Mazisi Kunene was appointed the

Chief Representative of the ANC in Britain and Western Europe in 1963. It was while he was serving in that capacity that I first got to know him. (Also *in Mazisi Raymond Fakazi Mngoni Kunene*).

Both of these statements affirm that Mazisi Raymond Fakazi Mngoni Kunene was a great poet, a progressive intellectual and a central member of the liberation struggle against white supremacy and apartheid domination. Through his poetic genius and his full participation in the democratic struggle, he represented the noblest traditions and aspirations of African people. It is for these achievements that the Nation bestowed on him the mantle of National Poet.

Given Mazisi Kunene's massive contribution to both Anglophone African literature and African literature in the indigenous African languages, would you encourage the creation or adoption of a course in universities or African studies programs in the continent and abroad to encourage research and study of his corpus?

When one mentions the colossal nature of Mazisi Kunene's productivity, many people are in disbelief regarding his monumental achievement. They regard it as impossible or unachievable. When I was a graduate student at UCLA (University of California in Los Angeles) in the mid 1970s and he was a Professor of African Languages at this institution, Mazisi Kunene constantly mentioned to me each time we practically met every day on campus that he intended to leave an enormous heritage for the Nation (South Africa) that would take decades to absorb and understand. He would tell me point blank that no one like him has appeared before in South African literary history, and usually when I heard this I would laugh and laugh and laugh! Despite the fact that I laughed and laughed, I took him very seriously because I could practically feel viscerally that he was enormously suffering because he believed, and rightly so, that South Africa was under "occupation" by European trespassers and the African people had momentarily been defeated. He had an unshakeable conviction that his writings would play a fundamental role in reversing this process of domination, at least on the cultural and literary plane. Mazisi Kunene felt so underappreciated by South Africans in exile, let alone those at home, and this thought invariably plunged him into deep depression many times. It should be remembered at this time that he had been defeated within the higher echelons of the ANC and had come to Los Angeles in voluntary exile. He viewed his stay in Los Angeles as a double exile: exiled from the country he loved, and exiled also from the political organization he dearly loved. But paradoxically this double exile enabled him to do something that gave him enormous joy: marry Mrs. Kunene to be and the four children that followed: three boys and one girl. Two or three poems in *The Ancestors & the Sacred Mountain* are about his family, most likely written at the time of his marriage and the birth of his children.

I think the reason that Mazisi Kunene was so productive is that he viewed himself as Geoffrey Chaucer of South African literature, or for that matter, of African literature encompassing the whole continent. He took seriously the perspective that the whole of African was a singular unified field force as evidenced by the statement emblazoned on the front cover of *Anthem of the Decades"*, *a* Zulu epic dedicated to the women of Africa. This astonishing fascination and preoccupation with Geoffrey Chaucer and *The Canterbury Tales* is evident in his major essay "Problems in African Literature" (*Research in African Literatures*, vol. 23 no. 1, Spring, 1992). Clearly, Mazisi Kunene viewed himself as an 'African' Chaucer because he thought their historical moments similar: just as Chaucer in the fourteenth century had struggled against the hegemony of Latin and made possible the subsequent efflorescence of English literature by writing his epic in *vernacular* English, likewise, Kunene viewed his mission in Africa as that of making possible the triumph of the African languages against the present hegemony of European languages in literary representation. Let me add also that undoubtedly the historical sweep of Chaucer's prodigious imagination was at the center of admiration.

I would like to indicate the scale of this achievement. Andre Brink and J. M. Coetzee in their anthology *A Land Apart: A Contemporary South African Reader* (1987) wrote that Mazisi Kunene was a "great poet" on the basis of his two epics (*Emperor Shaka The Great* and *Anthem of the Decades*) and two anthologies (*Zulu Poems* and *The Ancestors & the Sacred Mountain*). The quality of these four books do sustain this judgment. Brink and Coetzee, as well as many of us, could not have suspected the prodigious scale on which Mazisi Kunene was working. Research indicates that even during his London period, before his falling-out with the higher echelons of the African National Congress, he was already writing on a monumental scale, despite his many political activities. I had thought that this endless writing was only characteristic of the Los Angeles period of the 1970s and the 1980s. Probably in one of the earliest appraisals of Mazisi Kunene, a very astute and lucid estimation of the great poet, Mofolo Bulane reveals that not only was he writing a huge amount of poetry, but that it was being lost through neglect on the shelves of his apartment in London:

> Mr. Kunene has firmly established himself in the realist tradition. In doing so, he has not sacrificed the lively Zulu imagery at the altar of a fastidious demi-god of intellectualism. To the knowledge of the present author,

there is a lot of Zulu poetry rotting in Mr. Kunene's shelves in his London flat. This justifies Mr. Mphahlele's reiterated demand for publication, where possible, in African languages. Mr. Kunene is one of the most powerful and authentic voices in African poetry to come out of Africa in the past twenty years . . . One admires his guts to be indulging in 'poetic exuberance' considering the formidable task before him as a freedom fighter sticking to his guns in a grim political struggle away from the familiar South African setting . . ." ("Raymond Mazisi Kunene: The New Voice in African Poetry", in *The New African*, June 1966).

With the hindsight of history, approximately forty five years after Mofolo Bulane's brilliant estimation, Mazisi Kunene is probably recognized by many as the best poet to come from Africa in the twentieth century: in other words, arguably Africa's greatest poet.

To get a sense of Mazisi Kunene's overwhelming productivity, I would like to list the anthologies and epics that he wrote while in Los Angeles from 1975 to 1993, which I have extracted from his Curriculum Vitae that he wrote in 1995:

Poetry Volume I *The Wild Dog of Mhawu* (2210 poems).

Poetry Volume II *Mayhem in the Morning* (360 poems).

Poetry Volume III *The Smoking Pipes of the God Ra/Re* (276 poems).

Poetry Volume IV *The White Stone of the Mountain* (312 poems).

Poetry Volume V *The Spirits of Our Forefathers* (732 poems).

Poetry Volume VI *In Between the Nights* (31 poems).

Poetry Volume VII The Vision of the Diviners (908 poems).

Poetry Volume VIII *The Swirling Dust of the Ancestral Festival* (360 poems).

Poetry Volume IX *The Last Words of Khmet* (Egyptians) (224 poems).

Poetry Volume X *The Nameless Spirit* (150 poems).

Poetry Volume XI *Isibusiso sika Mhawu* (The Last Word of the Grandfathers).

Poetry Volume XII *Indiba Yamancasakazi* (The Circular Dance of of Young Women).

Poetry Volume XIII *Inqama Yas'Ekunene* (Sacred Ram of the Kunene House).

Poetry Volume XIV *Imyalezo yaba Chwezi* (The Last Mortal Embrace Of the Egyptians).

Poetry Volume XV *Amadlozi Obabamkhulu* (Ancestors/Forefathers).

Poetry Volume XVI *Ingqungqulu Yamalanga Amabili* (Two-Day Champion).

Poetry Volume XVII *Ubhedu Lika Matapa* (The Heroics of Matapa).

Poetry Volume XVIII *Ubuhlalu Buka Nomandishi* (The Multicolored Beads of Nomandishi).

Poetry Volume XIX *Ingqimphothwe* (Somersault).

Poetry Volume XX *Injongolo ka Mhawu* (Mhawu's Resolve).

Poetry Volume XXI *Zwana Elimnandi (*Enchanting Words).

These, presumably, are part of over a hundred manuscripts written in Zulu that I had the opportunity to look at when I visited his residence in Durban in 2007, a year after he passed away.

Given this extraordinary achievement, I would definitely encourage all Universities that teach African Literature to teach Mazisi Kunene on their curriculum. His four aforementioned works, which he himself translated, are somewhat readily available, though one or two are out of print. The translation of Mazisi Kunene's work from isiZulu to the English language was initiated three years ago by Macingwane Vusi Mchunu in South

Africa, who first met Mazisi Kunene during the Exile Era in the then West Berlin in 1987. Mchunu has just completed translating into English *Igudu likaSomcabeko* which was published in 1997 in South Africa; the English version should be coming out soon from Africa World Press. I have used the original and translation to teach Mazisi Kunene in the Department of Comparative Literature at the University of California in Irvine and at my resident institution, Pitzer College, here in Claremont, a suburb of Los Angeles. In the course on "Modern Black South African Literature", which I taught in both institutions, I taught Mazisi Kunene side by side with S. E. K. Mqhayi and Nonstizi Mgqwetho, both of whom wrote in their mother language which was isiXhosa, and have been amply translated in recent times. Teaching these major South African poets, who form the central canon of African Literature in the African Languages in South Africa, was a deeply moving experience for me. The students reacted with tremendous enthusiasm, which was very inspiring and encouraging.

What significance, if any, do you attach to Mazisi Kunene's return to South Africa in 1993 after several years in exile?

I think the return of Mazisi Kunene to South Africa in 1993 from Los Angeles was historically significant because in terms of cultural history it represented the closing or the end of the Exile Period in South African intellectual history, just as momentous as Ezekiel Mphahlele's self-exiling himself to Nigeria in 1957 opened this singular moment. The departure of Ernest Mancoba for Paris in 1938, likewise that of Peter Abrahams for London in 1939 and also that of Gerald Sekoto for Paris in 1948, were not that expressive of the country's historical imperatives as that of Mphahlele, since within three years of his departure so many members of the Sophiatown Renaissance (Bloke Modisane, Lewis

Nkosi, Arthur Maimane, Bessie Head, James La Guma, Dennis Brutus, Alfred Hutchinson and many others), of which he himself was a member, fled to exile as a consequence of the political repression that followed the Sharpeville Massacre of 1960. Mazisi Kunene himself was part of this huge exodus into exile, including also the distinguished intellectual and author of the great Xhosa novel *Ingqumbo Yeminyanya* (1940, The Wrath of the Ancestral Spirits), A. C. Jordan, who was a member of the "Magnificent Generation" of the 1930s (James J. R. Jolobe, John Henderson Soga, Mark S. Radebe, Herman Charles Bosman, T. D. Mweli Skota, James Calata, A. B. Xuma), a constellation of the Movement. The collapse of the Sophiatown Renaissance meant in effect the termination of the New African Movement whose emergence or existence was signaled by the publication in 1904-6 of Pixley ka Isaka Seme manifesto "The Regeneration of Africa". The Sophiatown Renaissance was the last intellectual and cultural constellation of the New African Movement. Mazisi Kunene himself belonged to the Zulu Intellectuals of the 1940s (Benedict Wallet Vilakazi, H. I. E. Dhlomo, Emmanuel Henry Anthony Made, R. R. R. Dhlomo, Credo Mutwa, Walter B. M. Nhlapo, Jacob Nhlapo, Anton Lembede, Gerald Bhengu, Kenneth Bhengu and many others) was one of the many constellations of the New African Movement during its duration or trajectory from arguably 1871 (the death of Tiyo Soga) to 1960. It is along this longitudinal perspective that Mazisi Kunene's return should be viewed.

Andre Brink's giddiness and enthusiasm regarding Mazisi Kunene's return was an expression of his estimation that in all probability Kunene was South Africa's greatest poet, which was all the more reason that he should return home, *heimat* as the Germans say. This ardent embracing of Kunene was evident in Brink's interview with him, which appeared, if I'm not mistaken, in *English in Africa* scholarly journal published at Rhodes University, Grahamstown in South Africa. It is possible that the interview was in the now defunct *Southern African Review of Books*. I would like to quote a paragraph from an interview Mazisi Kunene had with Zoë Wicomb, a distinguished South African writer, then at the University of the Western Cape, within a few weeks of his arrival in South Africa:

> First all I must say that I am very pleased and really very happy to be back in South Africa. I feel like I've peeled my mind out of some cave somewhere and I'm now out in the open. If feels fresh; it feels challenging; it feels very deep in terms of what one's responsibility is to one's society, to one's world and when I say world I mean the African world as a whole, of course, particularly South Africa because this is our home. We are all going through a process of transforming ourselves into a new world, a new kind of vision, a new kind of experience and finding answers to a lot of questions that arise out of our circumstances.

> ("Writers at Work: Mazisi Kunene", *Southern African Review of Books*, September/October 1993)

Although this interview seems to show that Mazisi Kunene had quickly adjusted on returning home, he was very apprehensive and very anxious about how he would be welcomed and received. His apprehension was in regard to the attitude and reaction of the political leadership of the ANC, given the fact that they had in a certain sense exiled him from London to Los Angeles. The literary establishment and the academic world welcomed him with open arms as is evident that he was given a Chair in Zulu Language and at the University of Natal (now known as University of KwaZulu/Natal).

The leadership of the ANC that was to assume state power the following year in the first democratic elections of 1994 never really accepted or embraced him. This is because Mazisi Kunene seems to have taken a neutral position when serious fighting which had the makings of a civil war broke out between the ANC and the Inkatha Freedom Party led by Chief Gatsha Buthelezi, following the release of Nelson Mandela in 1990 from a 27-year imprisonment. Inkatha fought on the banner of dubious Zulu Nationalism against the African Nationalism of the ANC. In the context of the impending civil war between Inkatha Party and the ANC, the leadership of the ANC became very suspicious and frightened of his political allegiance because of the following paragraph in the Preface to *Emperor Shaka The Great*:

> It is impossible to thank all the people who assisted me in this formidable task. I can only mention the few whom I think indicate the scale of involvement of people with different interests and skills. I thank particularly my brother and leader, Prince Gatsha Buthelezi, who greatly inspired and encouraged me. His glorious example of leadership is a true continuation of the tradition of his ancestor, Shaka the Great himself. Through such vision as he possesses, the actions of the forefathers became a living reality.

This was written in 1979. In these appalling and frightening sentences Mazisi Kunene was indeed declaring his allegiance to the Inkatha Party against the ANC. This was all the more astonishing since it was written down three years after Gatsha Buthelezi had used the Zulu miners in Johannesburg who were members of his organization as shock troops against the Soweto students who were leading the Soweto Uprising of 1976 against the oppressive apartheid state.

Since I left Los Angeles in February 1979 for Kenya, and from there to Poland and Germany where I lived for a decade, I did not come across the two epics, *Emperor Shaka The Great* (1979) and *Anthem of the Decades* (1981) until 1989 when I came back to Los Angeles. I had a violent quarrel with Mazisi Kunene about this paragraph. I met Gatsha Buthelezi once in 1977 or 1978 at his house in West Hollywood. In defense of this paragraph, which was in effect a declaration of war on the ANC, which Mazisi Kunene gave to me in our violent arguments, he made the unconvincing argument that since the ANC had in the early 1970s made contacts with Gatsha Buthelezi it was proper for him to embrace the "Prince". But the trouble with this disingenuous argument was that it had broken any relations with Gatsha Buthelezi after the Inkatha atrocities against the students in 1976. Equally dubious was to compare Buthelezi with Shaka! This comparison was a clear indication that Mazisi Kunene had lost his political direction and had entered a dark zone. After a falling out of several years without any kind of communication between us, Mazisi Kunene called me out of the blue to give a Keynote Address at a Farewell Dinner on the occasion of his retirement from UCLA in 1993. The Keynote Address I gave was entitled "The Return of Mazisi Kunene to South Africa: The End of an Intellectual Chapter in Our Literary History."

Given these circumstances and contextualization of Mazisi Kunene's return home in 1993, it is not surprising that it resonates on a multiplicity of levels, be they historical or political or literary. Perhaps for him the literary aspect was the most important, in that he wanted to be buried in the same national soil in which his four literary icons were buried: Magolwane, Mshongweni, S. E. K. Mqhayi and Benedict Wallet Vilakazi. I would like to quote what he wrote about each of them in his voluminous writings. Regarding Magolwane:

> Magolwane, Shaka's court poet, revolutionized Zulu poetry and created not only a form that was the highest vehicle of thought and feeling, but also evolved such a dramatic style of language that legend has it he needed only to beat the ground with his staff to emphasise the meaning of his poem . . . In his epic, he combined both

analysis and synthesis so that his stanzas not only introduced and treated the subject, but also contained philosophical conclusions and summaries"

("Introduction" in *Zulu Poems*).

Concerning Mshongweni, here is a tribute in a poetic form:

After the festival, after the feast

After the singing

After the voices have faded into the night

And the sounds of talking have ceased

And the angry winds have shed their manes

And the people have stopped to dance

Your voice and your voice only

Shall rise from the ruins.

Your dreams shall invade our earth

Creating an endless line of horizons

We too shall follow the song of the nightbird to the hill

The whole earth shall see the falling star

The time that bears the glorious seasons

Shall stampede to the valley of fruitfulness

The processions of the first-fruit shall come from all nations

The mountain springs shall burst open their freshness.

People shall thrust forward a movement

Like ecstatic minds at play

The future song shall be born

For the song is the sun of the earth

The earth is the mystery of the universe.

(in *The Ancestors & the Sacred Mountain*)

On S. E. K. Mqhayi:

Other African peoples of southern Africa show equal merit in their poetry according to the period of their history and national expression. For instance, Xhosa poetry has a rich tradition which was revived in more recent times by the great Xhosa poet, Mqhayi. The same can be said for Sotho poetry. The glorification of Zulu poetry as something unique should be avoided.

("Introduction" in *Zulu Poems*).

About Benedict Wallet Vilakazi:

As the Zulu literary tradition had been devalued, I started writing without models until I discovered Vilakazi's poetry. When I became dissatisfied with Vilakazi and others, I started my own metrical experiments based on the recurrence of stress in the penultimate syllable. ("Introduction" in *Zulu Poems*).

I would like to postulate that because of this great poetic lineage of African Literature in the African languages in South Africa, Mazisi Kunene wanted to return home and eventually be buried in the *national soil* in order to remain permanently connected to the *spiritual ambience* of this noble tradition.

Although undoubtedly the literary imperative was primary in compelling Mazisi Kunene to return home, there was also unquestionably the political aspect. His passion for politics never abated even though he was exiled from the inner sanctums of the political organization, as evidenced by one of the very few of his political essays that have survived the trauma of exile:

> The nature of oppressive regimes is such that as they grow more and more oppressive as they employ wide censorship on news and information reaching the country they control. Since the advent of the Afrikaner Nationalist Party to power, more and more laws have been passed to restrict publications.
>
> One reason for this is the belief that oppressed people will revolt not only because of the harshness of the laws but also because there is a collective sense inspiring such revolt. In a way this assessment is correct. All revolutions must by their very nature be a collective rejection of the oppressive regime. This sense of collectivity is achieved not only through a sophisticated underground communication system, but also through a sense of solidarity expressed by the outside world."
>
> (Raymond Mazisi Kunene, "U. N. and the South African Struggle", in *The New African*, December 1966)

The passion of this paragraph makes clear that he wanted to be present at the burial of Apartheid and at the emergence of a New South Africa.

The historical imperative for returning home was connected to Mazisi Kunene's understanding of the historical significance of Shaka to our history. Like other New African members of the Zulu Intellectuals of the 1940s, from H. I. E. Dhlomo to C. L. S. Nyembezi, from Benedict Wallet to Walter B. M. Nhlapo, from R. R. R. Dhlomo to Credo Mutwa, the towering figure of Shaka was inescapable. His engagement or confrontation with this towering figure elicited in him arguably the greatest essay he ever wrote. Excerpting just a paragraph from it is more than sufficient for our purposes here:

Few African rulers have been highlighted and made into a legend as much as Shaka of the Zulus. This is not only because of his own qualities as a warrior king but his genius as a military strategist of consummate quality. Shaka transformed the society and thinking of the whole central and southern Africa. In little more than ten years he had imprinted his political and military ideas in the vast region of southern Africa and prepared the regions for later confrontations with the invading whites. Shaka is perhaps the last of the heroic figures of past African history. Consequently his legend is not only alive as a political force but also as the mythic material of which histories are made. His role in recent history reinforces the validity of the continuation of African initiative, thought and institutions.

(Shaka The Great: Warrior-King and Founder of the Zulu Nation", in *Great Black Leaders: Ancient and Modern*, (ed.) Ivan Van Sertima, 1988).

None of the other New African intellectuals of this constellation wrote about Shaka with the rigor and conceptual depth comparable to that exemplified by Mazisi Kunene. I think the point here for Mazisi Kunene was that just as Shaka had *unified* the Zulu Nation, the ANC likewise had the capability of doing so likewise in the present context. Let me add quickly that by this time Mazisi Kunene had reconciled himself to the ANC intellectually and politically, if not emotionally. The pain that this political organization he dearly loved and had unreservedly served in Exile had not sufficiently appreciated his worth never left him. He took that pain with him to the grave. In many ways, therefore, the South African National Laureate Prize came *too late* for him to recognize and appreciate since by then his health had precipitously declined. Within fifteen months of this honor he was gone.

Mazisi Kunene was not particularly fond of the Sophiatown writing culture of the 1950s. Is this something you would like to comment on? Why do you think he felt this way? Do you think his views of this movement changed over the years?

One of the arguments made by Amilcar Cabral, the Marxist philosopher and revolutionary political leader from Guineau-Bissau, was that the violent entrance of European history into African history by means of the social system of capitalism and political institutions of imperialism and colonialism resulted in African people being forced out of African history into European history. This was the historical predicament of Africa imposed by European imperial order as it forced and marched the continent into modernity. Cabral also argued that a victorious national liberation struggle enabled African people to revert back to African history from European history. One of the intractable problems that European history deliberately effected through colonial cultural policy was the imposition of European languages on African languages. This resulted in the bifurcation of African literary history and the emergence in the nineteenth and twentieth centuries of two forms of *written* literatures in contention with each other: African Literature in the African Languages and African Literature in the European Languages. This bifurcation has unleashed one of the gravest crises in African cultural history practically affecting all African postcolonial states. This has resulted in the actual or seeming appearance of hegemony of African Literature in the European Languages over African Literature in the African Languages. African Literature in the European Languages originated with William Wellington Gqoba who was a member of the Xhosa Intellectuals of the 1880s constellation. African Literature in the African Languages, for all intent and purposes, originated with S. E. K. Mqhayi who was a member of the *Izwi Labantu* Group constellation. For Mazisi Kunene, African Literature in the European Languages is a "Literature of Occupation" because it embodies European cosmological systems and cultural values in opposition to African cosmological systems and cultural values. The logic of Mazisi Kunene's thinking on these contentious and complicated matters is apparent in some of his major essays such as "Background to African Literature", "Shaka The Great: Warrior-King and Founder of the Zulu Nation", "Problems in African Literature", "The Relevance of African Cosmological Systems to African Literature Today" and the incomparable "African Cosmology", all of which I'm assembling together in a huge anthology with those of the others members of the Zulu Intellectuals of the1940s. Given what Amilcar Cabral and Mazisi Kunene have formulated, I would argue that those writers who have been and are still preoccupied with African Literature in the European Languages are still residing inside European history, not in African history.

In parenthesis: The question of African languages will always be a contentious issue until it is historically resolved and the majority of African writers revert to writing in the African languages. The persistence of this issue is made clear by the publication of Chinua Achebe's *The Education of a British-Protected Child* (2009) about a year ago. Two major authors haunt this collection of essays: Ngugi wa Thiong'o and Joseph Conrad. Achebe continues his fight across thirty years against the position of Ngugi that African writers should write in the African languages as is evident in the several allusions he makes in several essays in this anthology without actually naming Ngugi by name. I would like to quote two paragraphs from one of the essays 'African Literature as Restoration of Celebration':

Some of my colleagues, finding this too awkward

[Ngugi's position that British colonialism as a matter of a systematic politico-cultural policy valorized the English language and suppressed the African languages], have tried to rewrite their story into a straightforward case of oppression by presenting a happy monolingual African childhood brusquely disrupted by the imposition of a domineering foreign language. This historical fantasy then demands that we throw out the English language in order to restore linguistic justice and self-respect to ourselves. My position is that anyone who feels unable to write in English should, of course, follow his desires. But we must not take liberties with our history. It is simply not that the English forced us to learn their language. On the contrary, British colonial policy in Africa and elsewhere generally emphasized its preference for native languages. We saw remnants of that preference in the Bantustan policies of South Africa. The truth is that we chose English not because the British desired it but because, having tacitly accepted the new nationalities into which colonialism had forced us, we needed its language to transact our business, including the business of overthrowing colonialism itself in the fullness of time. (p. 119)

Without going into the deeper complexities involved here, one or two things can be said. First: If the Europeans had to overthrow the hegemony of Latin in preference for their indigenous languages in order to become the Europeans they are today, why should that not be the case with Africans today! Second: It was the European *missionaries* who gave preference to the African languages while the European *colonial administrative system* in contradistinction gave priority to European languages. Third: Ngugi has never advocated the complete *elimination* of European languages in Africa, but their *marginalization* in preference for the African languages. Joseph Conrad haunts this book in a different manner. In about four essays in this collection he continues on his theme that he launched about thirty years ago that *Heart of Darkness* is practically a racist tract that does not merit the canonical status bestowed to it. In this book, Achebe sustains his critique of Conrad. The tragic irony here is that in his pursuance of the Anglo-Polish writer, Chinua Achebe has unbeknownst to himself practically transformed himself into a Joseph Conrad in regard to the African languages! This is said with the utmost respect for his remarkable talent as a novelist.

I make the distinction between *apparent* and *real hegemony* in characterizing the relationship between these written literatures because in South Africa in the history of the New African Movement the hegemony of African literature in the European languages over African literature in the African languages was apparent rather than real. Recent archival research in my country has revealed that New African poets who wrote in the African languages, from S. E. K. Mqhayi (*isi*Xhosa), Benedict Wallet Vilakazi (*isi*Zulu), J.J. R. Jolobe (*isi*Xhosa), Nontsizi Mgqwetho (*isi*Xhosa), J. S. Dlamini (*isi*Zulu), S. E. Ntsane (Sesotho), and Mazisi Kunene himself, were individually much stronger than the poets who wrote in English or in Afrikaans or in French in Africa across the twentieth century. Given this outcome in South Africa, I refuse to accept that poets who wrote in the European languages in other parts of Africa are necessarily stronger poets than those who wrote in the African languages, who are basically unknown to us, because no thorough archival search (in old magazines and newspapers as well as in archives) has yet been done. In this sense we still do not know the cultural geography of African literary history. Because of this lacuna in the investigation and mapping of African cultural history, I refuse to accept that the poets assembled in Gerald Moore and Ulli Beier's *The Penguin Book Of Modern African Poetry*, a book that seems to have become canonical on these matters, are necessarily the strongest poets in Africa. It is basically a faulty or a false canon. Concerning the novel in South

Africa, I think the three novels in the African languages, Thomas Mofolo's *Chaka*, A. C. Jordan's *Ingqumbo Yeminyanya* and S. E. K. Mqhayi's *Ityala Lamawele* can hold their own in comparison to the novels written by black South Africans in the English language and, in fact, surpass them. The presumption in my country is that the New African writers of the New African Movement who wrote in the English language were better or superior to those who wrote in African languages is false or very problematical at best.

It is within this context of the monumental cultural struggle between African languages and the English language concerning literary representation that Mazisi Kunene's persistent hostility over many decades towards the Sophiatown Renaissance writers who wrote in English should be viewed. He was very categorical that African literature in English written by New Africans was qualitatively inferior to African literature in the African languages. To him Sophiatown Renaissance cultural moment epitomized what he truly despised by designating it a "Literature of Occupation". I think what truly saddened and angered him is that the Sophiatown Renaissance had been given a canonical status by the majority of South Africans. He actually believed that it had little substance. He viewed it as a false triumph. I would postulate that he held H. I. E. Dhlomo responsible for this tragic situation. In the 1930s a cultural war broke out between Benedict Wallet Vilakazi and H. I. E. Dhlomo, close friends and both members of the Zulu Intellectuals of the 1940s, regarding which languages should be utilized in writing literature in my country. Vilakazi was the apostle of African literature in the African languages and H. I. E. Dhlomo was the advocate of African literature in the English language. I will not say much about this cultural conflict because I have written extensively about it elsewhere. In a recent essay of mine "New African Modernity and the New African Movement," which will appear in a forthcoming huge anthology *Cambridge University History of South African Literature,* I postulate that H.

I. E. Dhlomo emphasized in the 1930s African literature in the African languages his preference for African literature in the European languages. This explains Mazisi Kunene's hostility towards H. I. E. Dhlomo while recognizing him as a major intellectual. Simultaneous with H. I. E. Dhlomo undermining Africa literature in the African languages, Peter Abrahams brought the cultural achievement of the Harlem Renaissance to South Africa as though to reinforce African literature in the English language.

As we all know, the Sophiatown Renaissance of the 1950s practically came directly from the Harlem Renaissance of the 1920s. Though their actions were not directly intentional, there was a certain symmetry between the capsizing of one thing and the bringing of something as though to replace and reinforce something else. I do think it is merely accidental that Peter Abrahams in his *Return to Egoli*, consisting of reportages which he had been commissioned by the London *Guardian* newspaper to write, celebrated his intellectual comradeship with H. I. E. Dhlomo in the 1930s. It must be remembered that Peter Abrahams left South Africa in 1939 at the age of twenty one and came for a few months in late 1952, and left never to return again to present; he is presently 91 years old living in Jamaica. In all probability Peter Abrahams was sent to South Africa because of the Defiance Campaign of 1952. This book had an electrifying influence on Lewis Nkosi immediately on its publication. Lewis Nkosi was a protégé of H. I. E. Dhlomo. What Peter Abrahams was celebrating in regard to Dhlomo was their working as reporters in the 1930s in *The Bantu World* newspaper guided by the editorship of R. V. Selope Thema. It was Selope Thema who exhorted young African intellectuals in the 1920s and in the 1930s to emulate the New Negroes in United States in order to become New Africans in South Africa. Many, such as R. R. R. Dhlomo, Peter Abrahams, Peter Segale, Walter B. M. Nhlapo, Henry Nxumalo, Todd

Matshikiza, and H. I. E. Dhlomo, heeded the call. In the 1950s, Henry Nxumalo and Todd Matshikiza were to be among the dominant writers within *Drum* magazine, the intellectual and the cultural organ of the Sophiatown Renaissance.

I think Mazisi Kunene's hostility towards the Sophiatown Renaissance was an expression of his opposition to the nature of the whole historical trajectory of modernity in South Africa. As I mentioned earlier, he preferred a pre-modern poet like Geoffrey Chaucer, rather than the Romantic poets like Shelley and Keats respectively as Benedict Vilakazi and H. I. E. Dhlomo did, or for that matter, the modern poet like T. S. Eliot as Lewis Nkosi did.

Given all this, for me, the 1930s are more important than the 1950s in our cultural history.

Let's examine the agencies at work in Mazisi Kunene's corpus. Would you agree that myth and modernity functioned in his artistic appropriations and visionary commitments?

Although I have alluded in passing above to some members of the Zulu Intellectuals of the 1940s constellation, perhaps the best way to examine the agencies at work in Mazisi Kunene poetic *ouevre* is to name all its members in order to have a better sense of the intellectual and field forces that resonated at its center: Vusamazulu Credo Mutwa, Sibusisiwe Violet Makhanya, J. C. Dlamini, Kenneth Bhengu, R. R. R. Dhlomo, Gerald Bhengu, Emmanuel Anthony Henry Made, Jordan K. Ngubane, Anton Muziwakhe Lembede. Jacob Mfaniselwa Nhlapo, Albert Lutuli, Walter M. B. Nhlapo, C. L. S. Nyembezi, Rueben Caluza, D. G. S. Mtimkulu, Nimrod Njabulo Ndebele, Benedict Wallet Vilakazi, H. I. E. Dhlomo. It is possible to associate each of these names with the creative and political forces in contention at the time of its historical moment. Choosing nearly at random: Walter M. B.

Nhlapo---Popular Culture, Jazz and Mass Culture; Jordan K. Ngubane and Anton Muziwakhe Lembede, both founders with others of the African National Congress Youth League in 1943-44, consequently ideologues of African Nationalism which was first seriously theorized by Pixley ka Isaka Seme, founder of the African National Congress in 1912, in the pages of *Umteteli wa Bantu* newspaper in the 1930s, which they themselves re-baptized as 'New' African Nationalism---Ngubane practised great journalism in the tradition of R. V. Selope Thema and Lembede broached the idea of founding an Academy of Arts and Sciences which was originally suggested by Clament Martyn Doke in the 1930s; Rueben Caluza who struggled with the concept of modern music in relation to traditional music while equally fascinated by Negro Spirituals and Christian hymnology of John Knox Bokwe; Jacob Mfaniselwa Nhlapo was associated modern Education having been Principal of Wilberforce Institute in Evaton, Johannesburg; Emmanuel Henry Anthony Made a distinguished essayist, novelist and poet in *isi*Zulu about whom H. I. E. Dhlomo wrote two intellectual portraits; Gerald Bhengu who has become a reference point of *modernism* in painting within the New African Movement; Nimrod Njabulo Ndebele the first modern playwright in *isi*Zulu; R. R. R. Dhlomo was a historical novelist in *isi*Zulu about Zulu Kings from Dingane to Shaka, from Cetshwayo to Dinizulu; Vusamazulu Credo Mutwa has one way or another concerned himself with African cosmology, spinner of fantastic stories and tales; if I do not give particular reference here to H. I. E. Dhlomo and Benedict Wallet Vilakazi is because of the aforementioned intellectual duel referred to above.

Mazisi Kunene found himself in the vortex of this extraordinary galaxy of intellectuals. I would propose that being the youngest member of this constellation, the creative, political and philosophical practices of these figures imprinted themselves on his imagination, not in the sense of accepting or rejecting, but in the sense of *wonder* of what African culture was capable of giving birth to. I think this instilled in him an extraordinary belief that the African imagination was more than capable of achieving what the European was attaining. He repeatedly mentioned to me that all Europeans were *inferior* to him, with the possible exception of his beloved Chaucer. He equally mentioned to me that Apartheid was a sick joke played by Europeans with terrible consequences on us Africans. He told me that he would never write any poetry against Apartheid because it was below his dignity. He was very adamant with tremendous anger and bitterness certainly that Apartheid would be defeated in short time. At such moments I was genuinely convinced that he thought of himself as possessing the *visionary power* of Shaka. At such moments he would tell me that he was here in this world carrying out the edicts of the Ancestors. At this time I was about twenty six years old here in Los Angeles and he was about forty-eight years old in the mid 1970s. On hearing this I would smile and laugh but I always took him in earnest. I mention these things to indicate that he believed himself to be merely the *Vessel of the Ancestors,* concerning his imaginative powers. In fact, the last time I saw him in April 2006, four months before he passed away in August, when his health had completely declined and he was completely blind and could no longer speak, I spent four continuous hours just staring at him in his upstairs bedroom, just the two of us. Mrs. Kunene was downstairs with the Nurse Caretaker. He was really talking to the Ancestors and God (*UNkululunkulu*) in *isi*Zulu asking them "What was going to happen to the Children of Africa since the Hour of Reckoning Had Come." It was one of my extraordinary experiences. I wish I had a recorder to capture the profound things he was shouting into the infinity of space.

I mention all these things to indicate that the fundamental agencies in Mazisi Kunene's poetry were the Ancestors guiding his imagination to concern itself with cosmic forces that are at the center of the dialectic between Nature and History. For me the central text, as I said earlier, among his published texts is *The Ancestors & the Sacred Mountain* because it maps out the vast imaginative world where his powerful and formidable mind has been allowed by the Ancestors to explore the African cosmological world only a few in the African literary world, such as Mazisi Kunene and Vusamazulu [The Awakener of the Zulu Nation] Credo Mutwa, have been granted a permission to imaginatively experience. Compare the *visionary power* of Mazisi Kunene's poetry and the incredible stories of Credo Mutwa. At their center is the power of incantation, dissimulation and unfamiliarization.

Given your allusion to myth and modernity as visionary powers of representation, I would want to connect the material and spiritual to the ideological contestations within the intellectual history of the New African Movement. Perhaps Ethiopianism and Shembeism are central here because they were responses to European modernity's unending challenge to the African mythological world. Ethiopianism that occurred in the late nineteenth century was constituted by the breaking-away of African members from the European (white) churches in order to form their own Independent Christian Churches. This was truly historic because it represented what could be viewed retrospectively as the emergence of the incipient forms of African nationalism. This eventuation was truly a *massive national movement* driven by a totally un-theorized ideology which was to be systematically theorized many decades later, in fact in the 1930s, when African nationalism was in a state of war with Marxism. The founding of New African newspapers in opposition to missionary newspapers or of New African Associations and Societies again in opposition to those founded by the missionaries, was really a *localized* phenomenon even though it happened in many different parts of the country sometimes even in simultaneity with each other. Ethiopianism was a much more integrated national process. Its importance fractured the unity of the New African intelligentsia, with the majority of the members of the New African Movement opposed to it. The other importance of the ideology of Ethiopianism in the context is that it precipitated the fracturing of the New African Movement into two contentious factions: the *conservative modernizers* and *progressive modernizers*. The emergence of the *revolutionary modernizers* as a historical force occurred in 1930s when they identified with and appropriated Marxism in their struggle with African Nationalism of the progressive and conservative modernizers. By defeating Marxism, African Nationalism made certain that the 1930s would be one of the most important decades, if not the most important, in twentieth century South African history. The third item I would like raise in relation to Ethiopianism is that it was the first ideological connection between black Americans and black South Africans consequently making possible the first historical meeting point between the emergent *New African modernity* and the *New Negro modernity*. All of this is to say that Ethiopianism was in all probability inspired by the African Methodist Episcopal (AME) Church, a black separatist church movement that was established by Richard Allen in Philadelphia in 1787. The most radical leader in the late nineteenth century of the AME Church Bishop Henry McNeal Turner visited South Africa in 1898 to strengthen the relations with the Ethiopian Movement. Some of the New African conservative modernizers such as Charlotte Manye (Maxeke) and her husband Marshall Maxeke, before they were married, were educated at a historically black university, Wilberforce University founded by the AME Church, taught by a no lesser figure than W. E. B. Du Bois in the 1896-1897 academic year.

In the context of this question you have posed, I would say that Ethiopianism was definitely engaged with the *history* of South

Africa as the country was accelerating its modernization in accordance with the imperatives imposed by European modernity. Shembeism, which was largely confined to the Zulu Nation in Natal, was in many ways a continuation of the principles of Ethiopianism. A major contrast is that Shembeism sought to resurrect the philosophies and *mythologies* of African cosmological systems. While Ethiopianism largely followed the religious edicts of Christianity, meaning here Protestantism. Shembeism sought to forge a *syncretism* between African religious systems and Christianity. In many ways the African National Congress has always had to pay abeyance to the followers of Isaiah Shembe in order to consolidate and strengthen its support among the people of the Zulu Nation. I would partly attribute Mazisi Kunene's unyielding position on the primacy of the African languages over the European languages and his reconstruction of African cosmological systems to the contemporary legacy of Shembeism as well as, of course, to the great example of Samuel Edward Krune Mqhayi. The strength of the Zulu language today as testified to by two major daily/weekly newspapers in isiZulu (*Isolezwe* and *Ilanga*), probably a unique phenomenon in Africa, is partly a testimony to the power of this religious ideological system. Let me add in passing that the following week after the passing of the great poet in 2006, *Isolezwe* (August 25-31) published a splendid supplement appraising the incomparable legacy of Mazisi Kunene.

So definitely, I think African Nationalism, African Cosmology, the legacy of Ethiopianism, and Shembeism are the agential ideological and philosophical systems that profoundly resonate in his poetics. Of course behind them stands the historical figure of Shaka.

The name of Shaka reminds me of something I was forgetting. Since Mazisi Kunene was the youngest member of the Zulu Intellectuals of the 1940s, I enumerated the influences that were determinant of this intellectual constellation. In a lecture titled "The Transmission Lines of the New African Movement", which I gave at the University of Witwatersrand in 2006 and can be found on its Public Intellectual Life Project website, I postulated that there had been three intellectual traditions that impacted this constellation that made it arguably the most powerful within the history of the New African Movement: the Zulu Traditional Intellectual of Magolwane and Mshongweni, the New Negro Intellectual the Tradition of Booker T. Washington and Langston Hughes, and the Xhosa/Christian/Lovedale Tradition of Elijah Makiwane and S. E. K. Mqhayi. Each of the aforementioned members of this constellation reacted differently to this triadic force field of influences: Mazisi Kunene combined Mqhayi, Magolwane, Mshongweni and Vilakazi to make himself unprecedented in South African cultural history and second to none in African literary history of the twentieth century.

Political pressures in Apartheid South Africa forced Mazisi Kunene and several of his contemporaries in South African writing to seek refuge in exile. Do you think this decision affected his literary output and place in South African literature, considering the fact that writers like Nadine Gordimer who was privileged to live and write in South Africa as an ANC member never considered the option of exile?

It is interesting that you should pair these strong writers together because in their particular way they fought valiantly against oppression in my country, particularly against apartheid. Undoubtedly, the exile experience had a profound effect on Mazisi Kunene as I have already alluded above. At the height of the seemingly invincibility of the apartheid regime in the 1970s, before the Soweto Uprising of 1976 led by the students indicated otherwise, he mentioned to me repeatedly that the apartheid regime's occupation of the country was definitely a passing phenomenon. Mazisi Kunene had utter contempt for white supremacy's occupation of the country. The violence of this hatred really shocked me because it came from such a gentle person, truly one of the kindest people I have ever been privileged to meet. His rage and anger was so strong that he told me that it was below contempt for him to write poetry denouncing apartheid. I have not as yet seen one poem of his denouncing apartheid in a direct manner or in a sloganeering fashion. He was ambivalent about if not hostile to "Protest Literature". He understood the pain that necessitated protesting but nonetheless he thought it dealt with the mere surface of things not with the real spiritual and historical forces that undergirded this clash of political visions. Because of his extraordinary alignment with African cosmological systems, he was convinced that all physical entities in the universe were suffused with spiritual forces. For him the fundamental issue was the relation or the interpenetration or the intersection of *history* and *nature*. He looked askance at Marxism, not only because he believed it was a foreign ideology occupying Africa, but also because he believed it was the latest philosophical version European Enlightenment that subscribed to the domination of natural history by human history: what he strongly believed was the metaphysical reciprocity between the two. This is what is at the centre of his great essay on African Cosmology. I believe that the great poet went to his grave absolutely convinced that eventually African cosmology will eventually triumph over Christianity, Islam and other modern European philosophical systems that were presently occupying Africa. For him, the subordination of African languages to European languages in *modern literary expressiveness* was a direct process or consequence of philosophical occupation of Africa. So, definitely his extraordinary productivity in all probability, without precedence or parallel from a singular African producer, was the index of the painfulness of his exile experience. I have no doubt whatsoever that when the prodigious nature of this productivity is eventually revealed in its totality through publication to posterity, it will truly astonish everyone. I mean everyone, and even those who would not want to acknowledge it as such.

Now to Nadine Gordimer: this woman is extraordinary in her own manner by any measure. I would not characterize her having remained in South Africa rather than being forced into exile as the result of her having being endowed with a "privileged" status because of her whiteness or Jewishness. No doubt it was her choice to remain and fight apartheid and white supremacy from within rather than from outside. She did wage an unrelenting war against apartheid, like many other patriotic and progressive fellow compatriots. She did this in the public sphere of cultural politics by joining cultural associations and writers organizations which were multi-racial and most of which were subsequently banned. Her consequential effect on South African cultural history has been enormous. First, she was a member of the Sophiatown Renaissance of the 1950s, which was the last constellation of the New African Movement. At the center of the Renaissance were *Drum* writers, journalists and photographers such as Ezekiel Mphahlele, Lewis Nkosi, Bloke Modisane, Harry Bloom, G. R. Naidoo, Henry Nxumalo, Lionel Ostendorp, Victor Xashimba, Jürgen Schadeberg, Bessie Head, Alf Kumalo. There were also non-*Drum* intellectuals and artists of the Renaissance: Ruth First, Athol Fugard, Noni Jabavu, Christopher Gell, Alfred Hutchinson, David Goldblatt, Gibson Kente, Robert Sobukwe, Nadine Gordimer, Cosmo Pieterse. There were also British and American members of the Renaissance: Anthony Simpson, Trevor Huddleston, Lionel Rogosin. The Renaissance itself began in 1951 with the launching of *Drum* magazine and met its demise because of the apartheid state repression in the aftermath of the Sharpeville

Massacre of 1960. It was in this context that many intellectuals and writers fled into exile. Nadine Gordimer is one of the major members of this constellation who decided to remain at home. Her decision to remain rather than join the exodus has had profound positive effects on South African intellectual and cultural history. I consider Nadine Gordimer and Ezekiel Mphahlele to be the Last New African Intellectuals of the New African Movement, because with the collapse of the Sophiatown Renaissance the Movement itself came to an end which had defined South African intellectual and cultural history for half a century and its emergence having been signaled by Pixley ka Isaka Seme in 1904-6.

Second, by remaining at home rather than decamping for exile, Nadine Gordimer made herself significant through intellectual activity with fundamental historical link between the ruptured successive periods, the New African Movement from 1904 to 1960, and the Interregnum Period from 1960 to 1994, whose designation she invented in the great essay ("Living in the Interregnum", *New York Review of Books*, January 20, 1983; later assembled in her book *The Essential Gesture: Writing, Politics and Places*, 1989). When many *Drum* writers went into exile, one of the few members who remained behind was Nat Nakasa, who was perhaps the youngest member of this group. Before himself leaving for exile in 1964 and his subsequent tragic death the following year in New York City, he started a journal called *The Classic*. Nadine Gordimer was his principal helper in running the journal. Some of the writers who were to become important in the Interregnum Period such Mongane Wally Serote and Sipho Sepamla were to be inspired and encouraged into becoming writers by this journal. When these writers and others rejected fraternizing with progressive white intellectuals because of the ideology of Black Consciousness to which they subscribed, Nadine Gordimer respected their political position even though she fundamentally disagreed with this new form of separatism. In this real sense, Nadine Gordimer was the link between the *Staffrider* magazine writers like Sipho Sepamla, Njabulo Ndebele, Mbulelo Mzamane, Miriam Tlali, Mtutuzeli Matshoba, Mothobi Mutloatse, Achmat Dangor, Ahmed Essop, Mongane Wally Serote and the New African intellectuals and writers such H. I. E. Dhlomo, Solomon Plaatje, Peter Abrahams, Harold Cressy, A. C. Jordan and many others. To me, because of this, her contribution has been fundamental.

Lastly, as I argued in a recent of essay of mine on Njabulo Ndebele ("The Historical and Literary Moment of Njabulo S. Ndebele", in *English in Africa*, vol. 36 no. 1, May 2009), in my estimation, Nadine Gordimer was the person who transformed in the Interregnum Period the concept of the New Africa Intellectual to that of Public Intellectual which has proven so vital in the post 1994 period. In a lecture ("From H. I. E. Dhlomo to Nadine Gordimer: The Transformation of the concept of the New African Movement into the notion of Public Intellectual") that I'm presently preparing to give at home later this year, I attempt to trace how Nadine Gordimer achieved this monumental transformation. This is no mean achievement. To me, Njabulo Ndebele is the most important Public Intellectual of our moment.

In this cataloguing, I'm not even mentioning her great creative work that deservedly won her a Nobel Prize in Literature in 1991.

Social and political themes as freedom, justice, and morality remain some of the highlights of Mazisi Kunene's poetry? Do you think post colonialism and imperialism had anything to do with this?

It is difficult for me to characterize Mazisi Kunene's political philosophy in a concrete way and in a specific manner. It dawns on me now stemming from your question that I cannot recall in the thirty odd years I knew him ever asking about his political beliefs. His cosmological beliefs were absolutely clear because he did talk quite often about his connection to the Ancestral world. I just understood intuitively that his relation to the great nineteenth century poets Mshongweni and Magolwane was not metaphysical or merely the inheritance of a literary lineage, but was felt as a profoundly spiritual one at a deeply personal level. Although it was a given that he hated imperialism and colonialism, I never knew his take on Christianity. I do not want here to confuse the doctrines of Christianity with the role of the European missionaries in their "civilizing mission" in Africa. I knew that he despised missionaries because he said so to me on many occasions. But I do not want to imbricate the messengers with the message. I think everyone who met Mazisi Kunene would testify that he was an extraordinarily spiritual person. I do not know how his spirituality was connected to his religiosity, if there was any connection at all. I think I understand the connection or the integrated nature between the two within his cosmological world, but not their relation within the purview of Christianity. Thinking of the great poet, from the perspective of my entering the early stages of old age, I think he experienced his modernity in an uncompromisingly tragic manner. All of this is to say that I viewed him as a complex and complicated African nationalist. I would also wish to characterize him as a social democrat, given his passion for egalitarianism. Without him having said so in many words, being circumspect since we were in exile, I just knew that he had no time for Marxism and Communism, without him being actively hostile in regard to them. What was clear to me was his utter hostility to Liberalism. A serious study of his daunting monumental work will one day enlighten us on these issues. I think the best way to convey the political themes or issues that possibly guided his political vision is by quoting pertinent paragraphs from his essays that were written in a political mode.

There are several of these notations.

As a European representative of African National Congress covering the *whole* of Europe in the early years of the organization in exile, he gave the presentation to a forum whose provenance is unknown to us today, in which he said the following among other things:

> The nature of oppressive regimes is such that as they grow more and more oppressive as they employ wide censorship on news and information reaching the country they control. Since the advent of the Afrikaner Nationalist party to power, more and more laws have been passed to restrict publications. One reason for this is the belief that oppressed people will revolt not only because of the harshness of the laws but also because there is a collective sense inspiring such revolt. In a way this assessment is correct. All revolutions must by their very nature be a collective rejection of the oppressive regime. This sense of collectivity is achieved not only through a sophisticated underground communication system, but also through a sense of solidarity expressed by the outside world . . . Many a revolution has slowed up almost to a halt by its isolation. If a revolution is in essence an action carried out by a whole people, it is necessary to recognize that the dictates of revolutionary organization involve revolutionary zeal, realities of disillusionment, realities of mental isolation, etc. For these reasons also, the UN, in spite of its feeble position, can be used to benefit the South African revolutionary effort. This does not mean that the country must be sold to the UN or to South African liberals, who will be only happy to see a partial victory . . . The battlefield for the South African revolution is neither in Britain, France nor the UN, but in South Africa itself.

> ("United Nations and the South African Struggle", *The New African*, December 1966).

In his enthusiastic review of Mary Benson's *African Patriots* (1963), the first serious study of the political history of the African National Congress, Mazisi Kunene reveals what could be viewed as his political philosophy:

> In this historical description of the development of the African National Congress, one of the oldest African organisations in Africa and one which has consistently fought against racism and oppression, Miss Benson shows that the feeling of pan-Africanism and internationalism was evident in the African of South Africa as early as 1919. She succeeds by her remarkable insight into character to make the struggle of the peoples of South Africa live. One is amazed at the stock of knowledge she has of individual leaders who constituted the Congress leadership.

> No wonder, Miss Benson, knows many of the leaders in the turbulent history of South Africa, who have become her friends...She rightly states that Congress's greatest contribution to South Africa is its humanism. For the same reason she shows this nationalism as progressive as opposed to the "reactive" nationalism of splinter groups, indeed as opposed to the parochial and exclusive nationalism of the Afrikaner nationalists. For the first time we get a book which will show in later years how in spite of the selfishness of the ruling minority Governments, the African National Congress offered the only basis for a healthy South Africa. That the Governments have not taken heed of this voice demanding equality of peoples, is certainly not to their credit. ("A Healthy Basis", *The New African*, 17 August 1963).

Given what Mazisi Kunene writes here, the ideology of Humanism was one of the philosophical perspectives informing his political vision.

In another presentation given at one of the many international forums he attended as the European representative of the African National Congress (actually this address was given at the First Pan-African Cultural Festival held in Algiers in 1969), Mazisi Kunene had opportunity to express his hope that the political revolution and the cultural revolution would reinforce each other in the liberation struggle initiated by the organization:

Much has been said in this Symposium about the fundamental synthesis between the cultures, economics and the political life of the people. This is contained in the speech of the President and was also mentioned by other participants. This integration of culture in life and politics is a fact. As such one would have thought it unnecessary to mention. It is as if one would say all the participants here have hands which are an integral part of their bodies. But this is precisely the point.

Colonial ideology has atrophied our cultural limbs and in their place seeks to put artificial ones. This way it hopes to separate the herd from the elite, the barbaric and illiterate mass from the "elegant" intellectuals. Yet the pre-colonial history of Africa, whatever defects it had, preached emphatically an integrated ideology of culture, economics and politics. This is illustrated by a highly socialized artistic and literary tradition. From this tradition springs the source and stimulus of our creativity. We are therefore, in launching our revolution, setting out to recover these values and to reshape them according to the needs of our current experience. This is not in order to intellectualise our achievements, but to reinforce ourselves for the struggle for liberation and reconstruction. It is therefore essential to understand all the dimensions of African culture. Otherwise we shall remain a people uncertain and unable to make fundamental decisions relating to our future. It is part of this disease to indulge in ideologies which are essentially reactionary and prostrate before the colonial doctrines.

In this context, therefore, I would like to make an attempt to define that dimension. In defining, I must warn those who consider technology as the only criterion for achievement. I would like to warn them because of the persuasiveness and the ruthlessness with which this argument is bandied about, so much so that some find difficulty in conceiving of an alternative system of values other than that defined by the monolithic civilization of technologists . . . In short, the very idea of African unity is not a myth nor a political expediency, but evolves from very deep and fundamental experiences of our ancestors. I regard myself therefore as an inheritor of a vast and varied culture which our ancestors built. I am called upon to reshape and reorganize this culture according to my current experiences. This cultural festival assumes significance in this context in that it unites and provides an opportunity to share in the variety of cultures on this continent. I do not think Africans are superior or different from other human beings, but I do recognize the particularity of their contribution in the universal context. It is for that reason that I see our fate as very closely tied up with other human beings in this planet. It is also for this reason that I consider our tasks in recreating these perspectives of our history as a profound challenge. We are part of revolutions taking place not only in Africa but in Asia, Latin America and Europe.

("Revolutionary Challenges and Cultural Perspectives", in *New African Literature and the Arts*, vol. III, [ed.] Joseph Okpaku, The Third Press, New York, 1973).

Here Mazisi Kunene, in a most extraordinary way, was formulating a thesis of the historical imperative that the creative process must itself be a cultural revolution that affects all the domains of social life. The intensity of his hostility and opposition to colonialism and imperialism is apparent.

At the same time as he was formulating these radical political perspectives and revolutionary cultural imperatives, Mazisi Kunene was writing volumes and volumes of poetry that were undoubtedly solidifying his position a major figure in the twentieth century poetry. The first serious appraisal of him on the basis of poetry that was published in magazines such *Lotus: The Journal of Afro-Asian Writing*, appeared before his first book of poetry was published: *Zulu Poems* (1970). Mofolo Bulane, who was then studying at the Friendship University in Moscow, made this assessment:

> Upon reading Mr. Kunene's poems, one immediately discovers that there is a poet, the secret of whose charming and touching verse is its simplicity, clarity and originality. To those who know him, the poet in question has never failed to win admiration because of his simplicity. He is not, like so many of us mentally castrated in the Western tradition, a caricature of European culture. This is clearly demonstrated by the idiom and cadence of his poems which are steeped in the traditional Zulu oral poetry: apt lyrical associations interspersed with images from the sonorous world of the Zulu heroic epic. As we shall shortly see, he invokes the familiar landscape of the land of Shaka, with word-pictures that are not mere structures superimposed over the overall piece of exotica. Rather they are associated with the deepest thoughts of the poet's people, with the sentiments of the land to which he is first and foremost, addressing himself. They may be concrete place-names and proper names of historical significance; or some other phenomena that have come to be accepted as expressive of the best in human nature or the worst in life. But all these do undergo a complicated process in the creative mind of the poet. [When] they finally come out on paper, they are closely and fittingly [knitted] into the mosaic of words that transport ideas and aspirations and force a corresponding reaction on the part of the reader . . . Mr. Kunene has firmly established himself in

the realist tradition. In doing so, he has not sacrificed the lively Zulu imagery at the altar of a fastidious demi-god of intellectualism. To the knowledge of the present author, there is a lot of Zulu poetry rotting in Mr. Kunene's shelves in his London flat. This justifies Mr. Mphahlele's reiterated demand for publication, where possible, in African languages. Mr. Kunene is one of the most powerful and authentic voices in African poetry to come out of Africa in the past twenty years.

("Raymond Mazisi Kunene: The New Voice in African Poetry", *The New African*, June 1966).

In subsequent years Professor Bulane was to distinguish himself by writing path-breaking essays on African Literature in the African languages in reputable scholarly journals such as *African Arts* at the University of California in Los Angeles (UCLA) to *Pula* at the University of Lesotho.

Given Mazisi Kunene's uncompromising devotion to writing in African language until his passing, do you think such a stance will in anyway diminish his importance as one of the most important voices of post colonial/modern African poetry?

Even though Mazisi Kunene in the 1960s was the *only* one among the major African writers of his generation who espoused and actually practiced the cause of African literature in the African languages, he was absolutely convinced that he would eventually prevail against *all* of his contemporaries who extolled and practiced the cause of African literature in the European languages. In the latter group he included all those writers, poets and literary scholars who had participated in the infamous 1962 Kampala Conference of African Writers in English Expression that unanimously endorsed the writing of African literature in the

European languages: Bloke Modisane, Christopher Okigbo, Lewis Nkosi, Chinua Achebe, Ezekiel Mphahlele, Wole Soyinka, Ngugi wa Thiong'o (then James Ngugi), Bernard Fonlon, Rajat Neogy. Obi Wali, then a doctoral student at Northwestern University, wrote a dissenting letter against this view to the *Transition* magazine based in Kampala, Uganda. Mphahlele and Soyinka subsequently wrote ill-tempered and condescending rejoinders in *Transition* against Obi Wali. There was symmetry between the positions of Wali and Kunene. Mazisi Kunene was contemptuous of the Kampala Conference position and told me so repeatedly in Los Angeles in the 1970s and in West Berlin in the 1980s and expressed surprise why these writers would do so when in his estimation the major African writers of the preceding generation wrote in the African languages: D. O. Fagunwa in Yoruba in Nigeria and Shabaan Roberts in Swahili in East Africa. In South Africa there is a much more extensive catalogue of this literature: S. E. K. Mqhayi, J. J. R. Jolobe, Guybon Bundlwana Sinxo in *isi*Xhosa; Thomas Mofolo, Everritt Lechesa Segoete, Zakea D. Mangoaela in Sesotho; Benedict Wallet Vilakazi, Emman A. Made, R. R. R. Dhlomo in *isi*Zulu. Mazisi Kunene expressed his deepest rancor against South African and Nigerian writers who he felt had willfully misrepresented their own particular national literary histories. This rancor was evident in his dismissal of all the *Drum* writers of the 1950s as possessing little literary significance but only as court jesters in imitating and flattering Europeans; and his complicated estimation of Wole Soyinka's talent was evident in his appraisal of one of Soyinka's plays:

Wole Soyinka's play *Lion and the Jewel* has had various favourable reviews but one wonders why. This is a bad play. It is neither profound nor skilled technically. Soyinka has fallen into the trap of many present African writers who dress up poor skill with exotica...The conflict in the play is superficial...Technically the play is a failure...The play is disappointing since Mr. Soyinka is himself a good writer. The vultures who eat up everything African will eat even a carcase but the African writer must learn to detect these birds. They are bound to be his death in the end.

(Mazisi Kunene, "Soyinka in London: Two writers in London assess *The Lion and the Jewel*", *The New African*, March 1967).

Even though he would get depressed and melancholic when he thought about what he considered to be the *popularity* of the African writers who wrote in the European languages, he was absolutely convinced of his own greater genius, much superior to what he considered to be their estimable talents. He told me many times that his *genius* was not a personal achievement or possession but an epistemological tool momentarily lent to him by the Ancestors because he was in daily communication with them through the African languages (i. e. in *isi*Zulu). On present reflection, I'm convinced that Mazisi Kunene personally translated the epics *Anthem of the Decades* and *Emperor Shaka The Great* as well as the two anthologies into the English language in order to show the world that what it took to be contemporary African literature was in actual fact "exotica" in the European languages: his works had the cognitive wisdom, the aesthetic splendor, and the ethical values that characterize truly genuine literature as Harold Bloom argues in *Where Shall Wisdom Be Found* (2005). After these translations he went back to writing in isiZulu with the result that at the time of his death he had left over a hundred massive manuscripts of epics and anthologies. In other words, he took the *secret war* between African literature in the African languages and African literature in the European languages across the twentieth century in dead earnest: this is the real drama of African literary history in the receding century. He was determined to make the former prevail in the long haul.

To understand this remarkable determination on the part of this great poet, a particular episode in the history of the New African Movement needs to be recalled. This event was important in South African literary history. It happened among the Zulu Intellectuals of the 1940s constellation of the Movement. Both Benedict Wallet Vilakazi and H. I. E. Dhlomo, great friends but antagonists in this episode, as well as Mazisi Kunene, were members of this constellation. In the 1930s an intellectual duel, in fact an intellectual war, broke out between Vilakazi on the side African literature in the African languages and Dhlomo on the side of African literature in the European languages. Vilakazi seems to have precipitated the crisis in an article stating that African writers who write in English are praised by Europeans (whites) beyond their talent while at the thematic level these very Europeans refuse to accept these writings as genuine English literature; partly because of this Vilakazi calls upon these writers to return to writing in the African (vernacular) languages:

Many men believe that the real and only Native writers are those that treat their themes in English. This is a mistaken notion. A Native may be a prolific writer of diverse novels, books of travel, biographies and other small pamphlets published daily in English; but all this is not literature. It will find no place of mention in the voluminous *English Encyclopaedias*. As a literature all these books are a failure, but they are excellent and ambitious attempts. Our writers should revert into Zulu, Xosa, Sesotho and other languages and leave aside (not absolutely) these controversies about Zulu orthography (a subject I shall treat in the next article), and English and Bantu philosophies and psychologists---sciences which even the advanced Europeans fall shy to argue about, because they do not understand them. (B. Wallet Vilakazi, "Writers", *Ilanga lase Natal*, 18 December

1931).

A few weeks later Dhlomo responded by indicating he prefers writing literature in the English language because it affords him a wider access to a worldly audience, thereby making it possible for him to receive greater financial enumeration:

> In conclusion, I may say that though I, too, would like to see Bantu writers "inscribing" in their Native languages, I think they cannot help but write in English for two reasons. First they want a wider public and wider publicity (yes, of course, we want publicity---everyone does, whether or not they be brave enough to say so.). Secondly they want money---who does not? Now, if they write in Zulu, Xosa or Sesuto, very few will read their productions, but a good work in English will command, if not worldwide, certainly Union, recognition. (Does Mr. Vilakazi know of Mr. [Thomas] Mofolo's case in this connection?) Some may assert that I desire to sacrifice our cause for Bantu literature to mere personal gain. Not so. I believe that what Mr. Vilakazi terms "pure Bantu literature" can be produced even in England. To me it appears a matter, not of medium, but of the character, mood and nature of work itself. If white men write in Zulu, Xosa, or Sesoto, I would not say their work was "pure Bantu literature" for it would not express Bantu psychology, mentality, ideas, sentiments and aspirations. If by "pure Bantu literature" Mr. Vilakazi means writing in one or other of the Bantu languages, then, surely, he is guilty of grave illogic reasoning because it would mean that if I write a book in Zulu (I happen to be one) it would be classed as "pure Bantu literature," but when the same book is translated into English its English version would not be "pure Bantu literature," which, of course, is all bubble and nonsense.

> ("Mr. Vilakazi and Writers", *Ilanga lase Natal*, 1 January

1932)

This intellectual exchange between these major figures was one of the liveliest and consequential debates in our cultural history, preceded by that among Xhosa intellectuals between Elijah Makiwane and Pambani Jeremiah Mzimba in the 1880s in the pages of *Imvo Zabantsundu*, succeeded by that among Sotho intellectuals, chiefly between Peter Raburoko and Ezekiel Mphahlele in the 1950s in the pages of *Liberation* magazine and *The Bantu World*---all of them about the question of African languages in modernity.

As part of this ongoing discourse, in 1933 Vilakazi spelled out his allegiances by writing another article in which he stated his pride and solidarity with the Zulu intellectual culture that had been made possible by John Langalibalele Dube in founding the *Ilanga lase Natal* newspaper in 1903, an intellectual circle to which he had just been admitted:

It is only a year ago when you published in an article by me headed 'writers' and received a written frown from two writers, a Johannesburg 'Bert' [unbeknownst to Vilakazi this was H. I. E. Dhlomo] and a certain Mr. Nhlapo [in all probability this was Walter M. B. Nhlapo] of Durban. Because their words did not touch me I venture this year to approach the same subject from another angle and I hope I do not disturb the minds of my respectable friends . . . During my study I got very much interested in the writings of one 'Amicus Homini Gentis' [again unbeknownst to Vilakazi this was one of the other pseudonyms H. I. E. Dhlomo used] who as late as 1930 gave us his well selected notes that gave much variation among the writings of men like Rev. Dr. A. H. Ngidi who wrote very scientifically [had a column throughout the decade mainly about Catholicism and Roman Latinate literary culture] . . . Then becomes Mr.

R. R. R. Dhlomo [older brother of Dhlomo by three years] who has long patronized the paper and whose writings unto this day still hold good. One thing I like with this writer is that he is by reading a novelist with an open eye to everything that happens round him. He is also in political reports and criticisms. There is one thing he has not done the *Ilanga*---his short stories have so far not been published [actually they began appearing at the same time as this article in Stephen Black's *Sjambok* journal and in R. V. Selope Thema's *The Bantu World* newspaper for which R. R. R. Dhlomo was sub-editor of the Zulu section]. But why should he be so conservative with them? Do we not need them in the *Ilanga*? . . . Now I can say the *Ilanga* is dominated by the opinions of Mr. Josiah Mapumulo. Several times I have made mention of the name of this gentleman in this and other journals. We, who are writers for the *Ilanga* should copy this from this gentleman: To read and pore on books, and absorb knowledge from newspapers both old and new and never to say that we are grown old and tired of reading and reproducing. Many a time have I envied his quotations and wished I would turn a burglar to search his library of old books of history of many mission stations, both Protestant and Catholic [these quotations were as varied as from Sophocles to Terence, from St. Augustine to Pascal, from Shakespeare to George Bernard Shaw]. There is that lucidity in his writings which is unsallied with bias and uncramped by party opinions. His work should be continuous he must pioneer for the journal which is a living symbol of a black man's ability, the downfall of which will mean many lectures and newspaper articles on the failures of Bantu leadership in journalism. Black writers should defend us from many accusations laid upon us even very unnecessarily. They should weigh their writings before publication and assure themselves whether they are not actuated by self-aggrandisement or by fear of saying the truth. Writers in Bantudom are all engaged in the research work. There are books and historical opinions

we are out to argue against and overthrow altogether
because they lack substance or are overestimated. We
are now engaged in an age wherein we begin to want
to know the why and wherefore of everything.   (B.
Wallet Vilakazi, "What Writers Has This National Paper?",
Ilanga lase Natal, March 17, 1933).

There are several reasons for this rather long quotation from
this major Zulu poet, distinguished literary scholar, great
lexicographer, and close collaborator and close friend of the
incomparable Clement Martyn Doke. First, besides the three
intellectual traditions I mentioned above as having been
instrumental in the formation of the constellation of Zulu
Intellectuals of the 1940s, it is clear from what Vilakazi says here.
Also the modern Zulu intellectuals around *Ilanga lase Natal*
newspaper who preceded them, especially Josiah Mapumulo and
A. H. Ngidi, were also important in influencing them to being the
formidable intellectuals they were. I would like to add two other
names: Ngazana Luthuli, who was the editor of the newspaper
from about 1917 to 1943, and Robert Grendon who belongs to a
much earlier generation, who is presently emerging as a major
New African intellectual as a huge biography on him is about to be
published as well as his voluminous writings are poised to be
republished. Second, at the beginning of this intellectual duel in
1931-2, H. I. E. Dhlomo was seen as a more important intellectual
because of the remarkable articles, reviews and essays he had
published in *Umteteli wa Bantu* newspaper throughout the decade
of the1920s and in the early 1930s. Vilakazi must have been
viewed as merely an upstart without much to show for the bravado
that was displayed in the 1931 article.

But by 1938-9, at the moment their differences became
acrimonious and bitter, Vilakazi must have been viewed as an
intellectual on par with Dhlomo because of the Master's thesis he
had submitted to Doke in 1938 at the University of Witwatersrand

called *The Conception and Development of Zulu Poetry in Zulu*. Dhlomo himself wrote an appreciation of the thesis when its condensed version was published in *Bantu Studies*, the most prestigious journal in South Africa in the Humanities:

> In the first part of the work Mr. Vilakazi proves the existence of a great body of poetry in Zulu, dissects and analyses the form and technique of this poetry, interprets its content and recalls its beauty, fire and rich imagery. In part two he gives four divisions of Zulu poetry, suggests a term that covers the four parts, and examines the claims and achievements of the African tribal (or primitive) poet.

> Modern influences are discussed in part III. The study closes with the problems of the future of Bantu poetry. Here Mr. Vilakazi advances a new theory on rhyme system based on the phonetic relation of consonants of penultimate syllables, shows how scientific art is becoming, just as his thesis on the other hand reveals how artistic science can be. This rhyme system introduces a new element into Bantu poetry, and no African poet (unless he himself can advance another and as convincing a theory) can afford to neglect it . . . except at his own peril. Indeed in the light of this new theory many rhymed poems already published will fall under the re-sharpened scythe of the new school of criticism that Vilakazi has founded.

> The Bantu poet, I fear, will have no choice but to study the science of phonetics if he is to hold his own today, let alone [in] the future . . . Mr. Vilakazi himself has to be congratulated on being the first African---am I right?---to contribute a highly scientific and learned paper to a highly scientific and learned journal. Herby [H. I. E. Dhlomo], "*The Conception And Development Of Poetry in Zulu: An* Appreciation", *Ilanga lase Natal*, 20 August 1938).

Let me mention in passing that this appreciation as well as by Jordan Ngubane on Dhlomo's own epic *Valley Of A Thousand Hills* ("*Valley Of A Thousand Hills*: Story Of A Feeling, Hope And Achievement,"*Ilanga lase Natal*, November 29, 1941) were the beginning moment of serious literary appreciation by New African intellectuals within the New African Movement.

But inexplicably six months later H. I. E. Dhlomo wrote a sharp critique of Vilakazi's theory of rhyme, which he had earlier positively praised in the above quotation. I would like to quote the following sentences from it:

The question of rhyme is exercising the minds of those interested in the development of Bantu poetry. Rhyme can be an exacting taskmaster and a cold tyrant. Preoccupation with technique and rhyme may make for art that is too self-conscious. This is true especially of rhymes in African languages where words end almost invariably with a vowel, and where stress and accent play an important part in meaning. Here, rhyme may obscure meaning, stem the even flow of thought, and lead even to artificiality and superficiality. Our dramatists and "pure" poets are pioneers and innovators who are trying to find a suitable outward form for their emotional content. They would be well advised to develop as flexible a system as possible. In his "The Conception and Development of Poetry in Zulu," Vilakazi has worked out an interesting rhyme scheme. Actually, it is not new. Vilakazi has been forestalled by the European poets who attempted to develop double and even triple rhyme . . . Vilakazi pleads for a similar development in Bantu (Zulu) poetry. But his scheme is even more rigid and inflexible because the rhyme is not only double (i.e. beginning with the penultimate consonant), but is governed by the class of the penultimate consonant. Thus "Zulu" cannot rhyme with "mulu" for fricative alveolars have no ear-relation or even phonetic relation with nasal bi-labials. In this rhyme scheme, therefore, bilabial consonants can only rhyme with bilabials, alveolars with lveolars, etc. This is too rigid and crippling a scheme for dramatic purposes.(H. I. E. Dhlomo, "African Drama and Poetry", *The South African Outlook*, vol. 69, 1 April 1939).

What is fundamentally important is Vilakazi's strong response to H. I. E. Dhlomo because it reveals that an unbridgeable and traumatic split had occurred within the New African Movement between those who practiced African literature in the African languages and the practitioners of African literature in the European, and the possible effect one can plausibly presume it had on Mazisi Kunene. This is what Vilakazi partially wrote in this extraordinary response:

> By Bantu drama I mean a drama written by a Bantu, for the Bantu, in a Bantu language. I do not class English or Afrikaans dramas on Bantu themes. Whether these are written by Black people, I do not call them contributions to Bantu Literature. It is the same with poetry. For instance, a very excellent book, like Darlow's *African Heroes,* does not come within my category of Bantu poetry. It is a great book of poetry on Bantu themes; for that matter, English and Afrikaans books with Bantu setting, written by all our White friends are not Bantu literature.

> I have an unshaken belief in the possibilities of Bantu languages and their literature, provided the Bantu writers *themselves* can learn to love their languages and use them as vehicles for thought, feeling and will. After all, the belief, resulting in literature, is a demonstration of people's "self" where they cry: "Ego sum quod sum." That is our pride in being black, and we cannot changecreation.

> (B. W. Vilakazi, "African Drama and Poetry': Our

Readers Views", *South African Outlook*, 1 July 1939).

This passionate response is an index of Vilakazi's unyielding belief in the inviolability of African languages because of the African genius they enable.

Mazisi Kunene was familiar with this genius in the nineteenth century poetry of Magolwane and Mshongweni and its continuity in the twentieth century poetry of S. E. K. Mqhayi and of Vilakazi himself. His Master's thesis, *An Analytical Survey of Zulu Poetry: Both Traditional and Modern,* submitted to the University of Natal in 1958 or 1959, is a magisterial study of the genealogy of Zulu poetry from pre-Shakan era to the middle of the twentieth century. I would like to quote the "Introduction" to indicate the historical sweep of the undertaking:

There are two divisions into which Zulu poetry can be classified [traditional and modern]. These divisions, although not mutually exclusive, have specific characteristics which make them necessary. One type should be called traditional because it is uninfluenced by western forms of poetry. It is essentially an African art form. This type of Zulu poetry is related to poetry found amongst pre-literate people. It is an oral type of poetry having characteristics which are essentially those of oral poetry. As in all oral poetry, it has the same eulogistic tone, and seldom reveals a formal philosophical reflection of life. The reason for this becomes clear in the course of this work. For the present, it is enough to mention that poetry not being an isolated product is conditioned by cultural circumstances. Hence the poetic productions of the Zulus are expressive of Zulu culture in its different stages of development and change. Themes are based on the accumulated experiences of the Zulu society; ideas are expressed only in the form available to traditional preliterate Zulu society . . . From the earliest times to the present day Zulu poetry has continued to develop. To get a clear picture of what compromises Zulu poetry, it is essential that the course of its development should be carefully studied. In this work an attempt will be made to classify Zulu poetry according to specific periods which affected its development. This thesis deals mainly with traditional poetry as this forms the greater part of Zulu poetry.

Let me quickly add that Mazisi Kunene was familiar with other oral epics from other parts of Africa, especially from West Africa. He loved the epics from the Bambara people. But his favorite epic was *The Mwindo Epic* from the Congo. I know all this because I sat in his class for the whole Spring Quarter of 1989 at UCLA before taking the position in the Fall at the Claremont Colleges (specifically, Pitzer College): I had time to kill, so I thought that the best to do it was sitting in his course in order to see the master in action. Believing himself to have better knowledge of the history of African literature and its specific cultural products, he felt no compunction in criticizing those African writers who preferred writing in the European languages rather in the African languages.

I would like to conclude answering this question by indicating that although the issues of African languages and African literature in the African languages had been persistent throughout the history of the New African Movement, tragically with the death of David Livingstone Phakamile Yali-Manisi in 1999 and Mazisi Kunene in 2006, African literature in the African languages in South Africa may have died with them or may at least have seen its *last* major exponents. It was Clement Martyn Doke, the greatest South African scholar across the twentieth century, who fourteen years before Benedict Vilakazi in 1925 made the question of African languages one of the central projects of the Movement by writing the following:

Many centuries ago was propounded the old saying *Semper novum ex Africa* [something new always comes from Africa]. This has proved a true saying down to the present day, and, if South Africans would only realise it, it will prove true for many a long day to come . . . It may be asked: What are the particular subjects of study which are of such importance? I would suggest the following: the study of native habits and customs, psychology, religious beliefs, law, industries and social systems---all these would come under the general heading of Social Anthropology. Then there is the study of the numerous native languages, with attention to the phonetics, grammar, lexicography, proverbs, songs and folklore---these would come under the general heading of Philology. Further, there are the important subjects of Native History and Native Music. Here surely is a wide field of research, and one the mere fringe of which has hitherto been touched. But I am concerned here with Philological Research only, and that in the Union of South Africa alone. And yet, though this greatly narrows both the area to be covered and the subjects to be undertaken, there still remains a wide field of research to be explored . . . *I would digress here to make a plea for the recognition of the Bantulanguage family as one which can hold up its head with any other language family onearth. Bantu languages are extremely rich in vocabulary, and in grammatical, phoneticand syntactic structure, and their study presents a theme as noble as that of Semitic, Romance or Teutonic. But they have a unique grammatical system---one which it isimpossible to treat adequately except according to its own genius.* Hitherto investigatorshave come to the Bantu languages with the ready-made moulds of European or classical grammar, and have endeavoured to fit the Bantu languages into thesemoulds. The result is that much of the intrinsic beauty has been lost, and seemingexceptions abound throughout this type of treatment.

("A Call to Philological Study and Research in South Africa," *The South African Quarterly*, July 1925---February 1926, my emphasis*)*.

In 1932 in appreciation of the monumental work Doke had undertaken in studying African languages, S. E. K. Mqhayi wrote a poem celebrating the linguistic genius of this remarkable scholar. I limit myself to quoting these two stanzas:

Wambel' isimqe ukuya kuba Tshwana
Watat' umHlambeli no Makololo
Waya wadiba kowase Matshona.
Taru mfondini! Taru nzwan' enkulu'
Inzwan' enkulu encenywe yaneonywa,
Yada yanconywa nangabasutiyini.
Kon'ukuz' ibe neqeba nenxheba.
A! Zembe sangqingqana,
Igam' elibizwa yi Mbongi
A! Gqotagqot' inteto!
Igam' elibizwa ngasemva!

Ude wamtat' uXosa noZulu
Kok' u Xos' usuke watyyoboza
Kalok' olunye unyawo lusehlathini,
Ungabon' olo ngati lusekaya.
Ungabuzakoka Bene wokuxelela,
Kuba lo ka Ben' uzalelwe kona,
Litole lomtonvama kulo Jingqi.
Aw! Hayi mfondini ka Dyokwe!
Umz' ungxamel' ukuwuxakesisa!
Uwubope ngedyokw' ongazaziyo.
Yiva k'oka Plaatje uyakukalazela,
Oka Plaatje sitet' uTshekito.
Uti kowab' ilwimi zisawa ngokuwa,
Kowaboke kukweleba Tshwana.
Aba Pedi kawupind' ubazingele
        (U-Professor Doke", *Umteteli wa Bantu,*   1932).

Thus to the Tswanas he turned

He took Mhlambiso and Makololo

And back he went to Mashonaland.

Hail comrade, hail handsome one

The handsome man endlessly praised

Even by those of their fair sex

Who trade dry porrodge and mphothulo

That his stomach might bulge.

Hail!

The name the poet gave him!

Hail language investigator! The name used behind his back.

Eventually you ventured Xhosa and Zulu

But Xhosa broke loose

For Xhosa is not within easy grasp

Though this is seemingly not so.

Ask Bennie, he will tell you

For Bennie was born here in Xhosaland

He is the son of the amaJingqi soil.

Oh no! Son of Doke!

You have taken the people by surprise

You have tied them with a strange knot!

Hear how Plaatje complaints

The same Plaatje who is Tshekiso

He says languages in his country are still in a state of confusion

His country is Bechuanaland.

The Pedis say you should retrace them.

(Translated by Sidney Hudson-Reed).

Here is a partial listing of the books Doke published during the three-decade period of academic work: *The Grammar of the Lamba Language* (1922); *The Phonetics of the Zulu Language* (1926); *Textbook of Zulu Grammar* (1927); *Report on the Unification of the Shona Dialects* (1931); *A Comparative Study in Shona Phonetics* (1931); *The Lambas of Northern Rhodesia* (1931); *Bantu Linguistic Terminology* (1935); *Textbook of Lamba Grammar* (1938); *Bantu: Modern Grammatical, Phonetical and Lexicographical Studies since 1860* (1945); *The Southern Bantu Languages* (1954); *Zulu Syntax and Idiom* (1955); *English-Lamba Vocabulary* (1963); *Trekking in South-Central Africa* (1975).

There is no doubt in my mind that Mazisi Kunene was familiar with the scholarly work of Clement Martyn Doke for two simple reasons: one, it is inconceivable to me that Mazisi Kunene could have written his Master's thesis on traditional and modern Zulu poetry unfamiliar with a work of a scholar who not only championed African languages as well as African literature in the African languages but also was the dominant force in the study of African linguistics on the African continent; second, Doke was not only mentor, supervisor and later colleague of Mazisi Kunene's master Benedict Wallett Vilakazi, but also worked together (Vilakazi and Doke) in the work that resulted in the *Zulu-English Dictionary*, which was published a year after Vilakazi's death in 1948.

Given this long listing of Mazisi Kunene's cultural, historical, and emotional connection to Magolwane, Mshongweni, S. E. K. Mqhayi, Geoffrey Chaucer, Clement Martyn Doke and Benedict Wallet Vilakazi, I do not see how he could have been tempted in compromising his commitment to the genius of the African languages. He wanted to extend it further and further into modernity and postmodernity. Earlier I quoted Mazisi Kunene celebrating the literary generic form of the novel. Now I would like to quote him celebrating his master in a poem "A Meeting with Vilakazi, The Great Zulu Poet" in *The Ancestors & the Sacred Mountain*:

> Sleep tried to split us apart
>
> But the great dream created a new sun.
>
> Through its towering rays two worlds emerged
>
> And our twin planets opened to each other.
>
> I saw you descending from a dazzling hill,
>
> Your presence filled the whole world.
>
> I heard the drums beat behind your footsteps
>
> And the children of the south began to sing.
>
> They walked on the ancient path of the goddess Nomkhubulwane
>
> And the old dancing arena was filled with festival crowds.
>
> Your great songs echoed to the accompaniment of the festival horn.
>
> It was the beginning of our ancient new year
>
> Before the foreigners came, before they planted their own emblems.
>
> I came to the arena and you held my hand.
>
> Together we danced the boast-dance of our forefathers
>
> We sang the great anthems of the uLundi mountains.

Let me add something quickly about the 1930s regarding the Vilakazi and Dhlomo duel. I postulate in a chapter "New African

Modernity and the New African Movement," which I wrote recently for the forthcoming *Cambridge University History of South African Literature* (eds., Derek Attridge, David Attwell and Hedley Twidle) that the reason Vilakazi used such strong language against Dhlomo in the letter to the editor of *The South African Outlook* is that he believed that his friend had in effect capsized African literature in the African languages that had been dominant within the Movement from the 1890s ("Golden Age of Sotho Literature") to the 1930s (*The Bantu World* Intellectuals) and had in the process facilitated the emergence of African literature in the European languages which was to be epitomized and sanctified by the Sophiatown Renaissance of the 1950s, particularly by *Drum* writers within it. This is one of the reasons I think the 1930s decade, rather than the 1950s decade, was more critical in South African cultural history of the twentieth century.

In many ways I agree with Vilakazi in holding Dhlomo responsible for this because the latter from the middle of the 1920s to the end of his life was writing brilliant essays on literary theory, plays examining the past (tradition) and the present (modernity), short stories and the brilliant journalism which principally appeared in *Umteteli wa Bantu* newspaper from 1924 to the early 1930s; poetry began appearing in earnest in the 1940s in *Ilanga lase Natal* newspaper. The aesthetic power of this work in the English language debilitated the then hegemony of African literature in the African languages. Dhlomo was enabled in overthrowing of African literature in the African languages by R. V. Selope Thema's ideology of violently suppressing African tradition in order for modernity, especially that exemplified by the New Negro variant, to triumph. Selope Thema was the senior colleague of Dhlomo in their *Umteteli wa Bantu* days (1920s), as he was to be editor of *The Bantu World* in the 1930s, thereby commissioning many articles from Dhlomo for the newspaper. As editor, Selope Thema exhorted young African intellectuals to emulate the historical lessons of New Negro modernity in United States in order to construct an exemplary New African modernity in South Africa. At this time, Selope Thema as editor surrounded himself with very bright young New African intellectuals: R. R. R. Dhlomo, Peter Segale, Peter Abrahams, H. I. E. Dhlomo, Guybon Bundlwana Sinxo, Todd Mathisikiza, Henry Nxumalo, and a few others. Taking the ideological words of Selope Thema in absolute earnest, Peter Abrahams, before leaving the country permanently in 1939, for all intents and purposes, pulled the literary modernism of the Harlem Renaissance into South Africa as a kind of cultural excellence that had to be admired through emulation. Matshikiza and Nxumalo took the war words of Selope Thema to the pages of *Drum* magazine in the 1950s. Let me close by saying that Dhlomo did not endorse Selope Thema's hatred of tradition. Rather, he sought a reciprocal relationship between tradition and modernity, with modernity playing a dominant role.

Mazisi Kunene's respect for ancestral art forms is a major part of his vision. Why do you think he was persistent in this undertaking?

Mazisi Kunene exemplifies his profound and deep engagement with ancestral art forms in the earliest critical work and the only work in that genre he ever wrote: I'm referring to his 1958 or 1959 Master's thesis written for the University of Natal, *An Analytical Survey of Zulu Poetry: Both Traditional and Modern,* which occupies a legendary position in the history of South African scholarship. Many of my compatriots through reputation have argued that it is perhaps the best thesis ever written in the country in the field of the Humanities. Some have argued that it can only be compared with Benedict Wallet Vilakazi's doctoral dissertation submitted to the University of Witwatersrand: *The Oral Written*

And Written Literature in Nguni (1946). This comparison must have flattered Mazisi Kunene because he always regarded Vilakazi as his master: he mentions or alludes to him in Prefaces, Introductions to his work and has dedicated one or two poems to him. The brilliance of the thesis is such that some scholars have argued the chapter on Zulu Literature in Albert Gerard's landmark book *Four African Literatures: Xhosa, Sotho, Zulu and Amharic* (1971) relies too heavily on it. It was on the basis of *An Analytical Survey of Zulu Poetry and Zulu Poems* (1970) that Kunene was given a professorship in the Department of Languages and Linguistics in 1975, then one of the best departments in the world, at the University of California in Los Angeles (UCLA). One of its uniqueness is that at the time it was one of the very few texts of high quality on the literary history of African Literature in the African Languages. The earlier works of A. C. Jordan within the New African Movement, a Master's thesis and a doctoral dissertation, respectively *Some Features of the Phonetic and Grammatical Structure of Baça* (1942) submitted to the Department of African Studies and Languages at the University of Fort Hare and *A Phonological and Grammatical Study of Literary Xhosa* (1956) submitted to the University of Cape Town, were concerned with linguistics rather than literary history of literary criticism. It was the great linguist Clement Martyn Doke who dominated the study of African Literature in the African Languages in South Africa in the first half of the twentieth century who pulled this field in the direction of linguistics rather than of literary history and poetics. This is not to say that Doke completely ignored literary history and poetics because many of his voluminous book reviews in *Bantu Studies* journal (later renamed *African Studies*) were engaged with them. It is interesting in this context that Benedict Vilakazi wrote his doctoral dissertation under the supervision of Doke in the field of literary history rather than linguistics. D. D. T. Jabavu's *Bantu Literature* and *The Influence of English on Bantu Literature*, both published in the 1920s, and C. L. S. Nyembezi's *A Review of Zulu Literature* (1961), are brilliant pamphlets rather than extended scholarly works. Nevertheless, both of these latter works were part of a rich inheritance that informed *An Analytical Survey of Zulu Poetry: Both Traditional and Modern.*

In the Introduction to the thesis, Mazisi Kunene formulates the ambitious nature of his undertaking with these words:

It is proposed in this thesis to make an analytical study of both traditional and modern Zulu poetry. The survey will cover the earliest periods of Zulu poetry, up to the very modern period of recorded poetry.

There are two divisions into which Zulu poetry can be classified. These divisions, although not mutually exclusive, have specific characteristics which make them necessary. One type should be called traditional because it is uninfluenced by western forms of poetry. It is essentially an African art form. This type of Zulu poetry is related to poetry found amongst most pre-literate people. It is an oral type of poetry having characteristics which are essentially those of oral poetry. As in all oral poetry, it has the same eulogistic tone, and seldom reveals a formal philosophical reflection of life. The reason for this becomes clear in the course of this work. For the present it is enough to mention that poetry, not being an isolated product, is conditioned by cultural circumstances. Hence the poetic productions of the Zulus are expressive of Zulu culture in its different stages of development and change. Themes are based on the accumulated experiences of the Zulu poetry; ideas are expressed only in the form available to traditional preliterate Zulu poetry.

In a general study of oral poetry one could go so far as to say that there is a fundamental similarity in the use of techniques as, for instance, in the universal usage of repetition. The manner in which these techniques are used naturally vary from country to country and from time to time. Zulu traditional poetry, therefore, has its own specific characteristics which distinguish it from other oral poetical works.

From the earliest times to the present day Zulu poetry has continued to develop.

To get a clear picture of what comprises Zulu poetry, it is essential that the course of its development should be carefully studied. In this work an attempt will be made to classify Zulu poetry according to specific periods which affected its development. This thesis deals mainly with traditional poetry as this forms the greater part of Zulu poetry.

A historical account of the development of the Zulu nation is included as essential to the study of Zulu poetry. The very nature of Zulu poetry demands that a thorough study should be made of Zulu poetry; obscure facts can only be elucidated by historical accounts.

With the cultural impact caused by the coming of the European in South Africa, a new form of poetic expression has arisen showing a strong influence of western (English) poetry. In this period, re-organisation of society is followed by re-organisation of ideas. The impact of Zulu culture made by foreign culture was to stimulate a strong desire in poets to imitate. Some attempt to find a compromise between the traditional and foreign forms of poetical expression. As would be imagined, this poetry is composed by the educated African. Few pieces of this type are available owing to the difficulties of finding a market for African literature; the rest lies in manuscript form. The little that is available discloses interesting experimentation. Poets have experimented with rhyme, syllabic metre, and various stanza forms. On account of these experiments this type of poetry has been dubbed academic.

Traditional poetry has fewer enthusiasts than before, especially amongst urbanized Africans. Not only because an active foreign culture is more attractive, but also because the customs, the life, and the social organization that in itself inspired traditional poetry has changed. The result is that although its appreciation as a form of poetic expression still remains, it is based on traditional works rather than on original modern compositions. The compositions found in the reserves are in most cases modifications of traditional works and seldom original. Those that do exist generally lack the epic conception of traditional works.

Using one of the finest Africana Libraries in the world, the Kellie Campbell Manuscript Library, now part of the University of kwaZulu/Natal Library, Mazisi Kunene undertakes a comprehensive historical and critical study of Zulu poetic from the sixteenth century to the present (the middle of the twentieth century).

Although as much as possible he is conscious of the necessity of attributing the poetic form to particular *imbongi* (bards or poets), in order to understand the singular imagination of each particular creator, he nevertheless divides the whole history of Zulu poetry into three historical periods: Pre-Shakan Era, the Shakan Era, and the Post-Shakan Era. Within this periodization, he examines distinct poetic forms that in the process he historicizes: eulogistic poetry, lyrical poetry, dramatic poetry and elegies. Besides using the *written* material such as *Olden Times in Zululand and Natal* by A. T. Brant and *Long Long Ago* by Samuelson as well manuscripts at the Kellie Campbell Library, Mazisi Kunene also undertook extensive field-work in order to understand firsthand the *voicing* of Zulu poetic forms. What is so extraordinary about the thesis is its conveyance of the unmatched understanding of Zulu poetry Mazisi Kunene had. Its historical sweep across the ages is combined with the particularization and specification of poetic form to a particular historical moment. If nothing else, the document shows that Mazisi Kunene had a strong critical imagination in the sense that his criticism is about evaluation and making distinctions between excellence and mediocrity. This perhaps explains the strong judgments he made in his evaluations. What is so instructive about Mazisi Kunene is that through analysis of a particular poetic form he unfolds the social milieu in which such a creative process occurred. One feels a strong sense that in making these critical judgments Mazisi Kunene was already imaginatively creating the great poetry he was to actualize in written form in subsequent decades: in other words, the creative imagination and the critical imagination are inseparable from each other. This perhaps explains why Mazisi Kunene's poetry is so much preoccupied with historical divides: between tradition and modernity, History and Nature, the past and the present, the singular and the universal, the female principle and the male principle and so on. Despite this, one feels very strongly that he agreed with Stéphane Mallarmé's adage that poetry is constructed by means of words not ideas.

Mazisi Kunene divides the Pre-Shakan Era into two periods: the Pre-Dingiswayo Period and the Dingiswayo Period. Under the former period, he mentions the following Zulu Kings: Ndaba (1697-1763), Simamane (1650-1741), Mavovo (1718-1788), Jama (1727-1781), Khondlo (1753-1813), Jobe (1707-1807). In the latter period, he names the following: Dingiswayo (1748-1818), Senzangakhona (1757-1816), Macingwane (1775-1820), Zwide (1757-1822), and there follows relatively minor Chiefs (Sompisi Kaguqa, Mbengi, Nandi Kambengi, and Mkabayi Kajama). During the Shakan Era he names the following Kings: Shaka (1790-1828) and Dingane (1807-1840), some minor Chiefs (Sihayo Kamapholoba and Xesibe Kangwane Zondi) and Outstanding Women (Nozinhlanga KaseNlangakhona and

Masichazana Unina KamaQhoboza) and the Places sacredly associated with Shaka (Umuzi KaShaka Embelebeleni and Umuzi KaShaka KwaDukuza). The Post-Shakan Era was ruled by these Kings: Mpande KaSenzangakhona (1840-1872), Cetshwayo [ruler from 1872 to 1879], Dinizulu [ruler from 1884 to 1913], Solomon KaDinizulu [ruler 1913 to 1933], Cyprian KaSolomon [1948 to 1968] and the minor Chiefs, minor Poets and White Personalities (Mganu KaNodada, Mtshabi KanoShadu, Mkhungo KamaNqondo WakwaMagwaza, Njantoni "John Dunn", Somtsewu KasoNzica "Sir Theophilus Shepstone", Zibezu Kamaphitha, Mzimba Kadibinyika (1843-1898) and Bambatha KamaNciza.

When Mazisi Kunene eventually gets to the Modern Poets, he designates cultural periods through the names of the poets themselves rather than those of the ruling regimes or ruling personalities: Dr Benedict Wallet Vilakazi, Emmanuel Anthony Henry Made, Thos Mthembu, Elliott Mhike, Abner S. Kunene and J. S. Matsebula. For each historical moment, Mazisi Kunene undertakes a detailed historical and poetic analysis.

What I would like to do here is quote what Mazisi Kunene in his younger days wrote of Shaka and the great poet Magolwana who dominated this historical period.

Of Shaka, whom he was to immortalize in a literary form two decades later in *Emperor Shaka The Great,* Mazisi Kunene had has this to say:

Enough has been said about Shaka to give the reader an idea of what kind of a man he was [Mazisi Kunene in the Pre-Shakan Era and in the Post-Shakan Era sections of the thesis wrote extensively about the great ruler]. He travelled widely enough and suffered long enough to develop a broad mind. He was proud and sensitive. Continuous humiliation in his youth fired him with the ambition to "devour" all the rulers and make himself supreme in Nguniland. His greatness can only be appreciated when we consider that at the time he assumed kingship of the Zulu clan, the Zulus were a small tribe, depending on others for protection. His task was titanic. By great military skill he managed to conquer territories near and far. He made himself one of the greatest rulers in Africa---comparable to Attila in military skill or to Alexander the Great. These great military achievements stimulated poetry and music.

Of Magolwana:

A word should be said about Shaka's Court poet, whose name, at least, happens to be known to us. Magolwana is the greatest traditional poet. There is very little that is known about him except that he was Shaka's Court poet. It is related that whilst reciting poetry he used to beat the ground to emphasize the rhythm of his poetry.

His contribution to Zulu poetry cannot be overestimated. He perfected the stanza form. His poetry contains much that is admirable, as the analysis of Shaka's eulogy hows.

The poet in a highly pictorial language extols the bravery of Shaka and those national events associated with him. Note that although the poet praises his bravery, he is not praising Shaka the person, but Shaka the national hero. Thus he does not give tedious details of how Shaka killed those he killed. He gives their names and says just enough about the events.

Shaka's conquests are like a wild fire, says the poet. Nobody can stand this fire.

Even powerful chiefs like Phakathwayo have been destroyed. As soon as armies appear, women leave their hoes and grain baskets in the fields to flee. He is:

Uzulu lizayo khwezani abantwana,
Ngabadada bodwa abazozibalekela.

He is depicted as spreading his influence everywhere. He is the asylum of the   powerful Kings like Zihlandlo. He does not fight like former rulers who left their enemies if they fled, but he is:

Umxhoshi womuntu amxhoshele futhi,
Ngimthande exhosha uZwide ozalwa uLanga,
Emthabatha lapho liphuma khona,
Emsingisa lapha lipha lishona khona.

He is the dread of the country:

USilwane---hlelele.

The poet gives a series of names of the people whom Shaka conquered: Phungashe, Sondaba, Macingwane, Mangcengceza, Dladlana, Xaba, Gambushe and Faku. He realizes that it would be monotonous if he enumerated all of them at the same time. After all, they too were conquered at different times He talks about Shaka's merits. Thereafter, he constructs the most artistic and most effective stanza in all Zulu poetry, deriving it from Dingiswayo's verse:

Ngithe ngisadle ezinye ngdla ezinye.

He does say specifically which nations were conquered but to show   numerous the conquered were, he repeats the verse (ten times):

Othe edle ezinye wedla ezinye,
Wathi esadle ezinye wedla ezinye.

(Note that the poet no longer refers to conquered individuals but to nations. was 'eating' nation after nation).

The poet is carried away in ecstasy and freely indulges in romanticism:

Umasongo-mahle! Inkonyane yenkomo!

There is no time to waste on such personal references. The poet hurries to extol Shaka's elusiveness and his bravery that has been a boon to the nation. He has conquered Mathondo, Msikazi, and Nyanga. He leaves all houses of his enemies   ablaze wherever he passes:

Ohamba ebasa eshiya amakloba.

He confiscated all the cattle at Zwide's and drove them to his house at Bulawayo::

Kwakungasakhali-nkomo kwaNtombazane,
Inkomo yayisikhala kwa Bulawayo.

The poet likens Shaka to a thunderbolt that brought untold destruction to Zwide's troops. He enumerates twelve relatives of Zwide whom Shaka captured. The poet builds up Zwide's prestige by garlanding his name with the names of the famous relatives. The idea being that if Zwide was so powerful Shaka was almost super-human to have been able to destroy him. He calls on Shaka to halt, using the negative technique actually implying that he should go on.

The poet frequently varies domestic scenes with national events. This he does, no doubt, in order not to tire the mind with the narration of military events. The poet says Shaka became 'married' to Zwide's sister, whom he had captured after conquering Zwide.

The infinity of Shaka's conquests is inexhaustible. Now and then the poet returns to them. The enumeration of the conquered pleases the poet and also fills the nation with pride and reverence for the King.

Note that there is frequent use of compound nouns, e.g. Usihlangu- indaba, uSiphepho-shunguza, uMasukwana-kuze. Note also that the poet uses different verbs in the stanzas pointing out those whom Shaka conquered. The verbs used are 'eat', 'venture forth' and 'come with'.

After a long interval, the poet repeats his perfected stanza referring to endless conquests. He achieves variety by the use of a different subjectival concord in the first word of each verse:

Yathi isadhla ezinye yadhla ezinye,
Ithi Isadhle ezinye idhle ezinye.

The poet realizes that if he goes beyond five verses the stanza would lose its effect because our minds are no longer as startled by it as when we first heard it. He realises, however, its artistic merit hence he repeats the stanza.

In the next stanza his voice is almost suffocated by the

greatness of Shaka. He says of him:

Ongangezwe lakhe omkhulu kakhulu!!
Ongangezintaba ezinde!
Ongangezindude!
Ongangesihlhla esisokhalwenik' kuMaqhwakazi!
Esasihlạl' uNdwandwe namaNxumalo.

Thereafter the poet breaks the monotony of the usual direct method by making an address to an imaginary figure. The poet breaks down and weeps with inner joy that springs from the feeling that he is in touch with infinity. He says in the most tender words:

Ungisize Maphitha noNgqengelele,
Umnike-nkomonye . . . afunde ukukleza
Umnike ukhande lokuzimbela.

The joy of looking after infinity as if he possessed it as his own cannot last long. Soon he realizes that he is a dot in the universe; he is suddenly filled with fear:

UNdaba ngiyameba, ngimuka naye,
Ngimbuka kwehla izinyembezi,
Kube sengathi ngibuka isihlahla somdlebe.

The poet builds up for the climax by mentioning that Shaka symbolizes infinity:

Ongangezintaba ezinde.

Even after the climax of his ecstasy he cannot get over the greatness he has beheld.

He desperately tries to recapture it:

*UNdaba ulud

udu emanxulumeni,*
Ugungubele njengolwande,
Lona kuze kuse lugubhelana,
Isidlangudlandlu esinjengendlebe yendlovu,
Ongangecumbe yamabel' angadliwa,
Ongangembiza yamashongololo,
Uyisilo! uyiNgwe! uyiNgonyama!
Uyindlondlo! uyindlovu!

His attempt fails because greatness cannot be recaptured; he is drowned in it. It is only when he gains control of his emotions again that we feel greatness rumbling   under his verse. Shaka is:

Sidlukula-dlwedlwe siyadla sidlodlobele,
Sibeke izihlangu emadolweni.

In these verses one is able to perceive at least the outline of Shaka's form. When the poet says:

Izulu eladuma emaMpondweni,
Phezu kukaFaku umntakaNgqungushe,

He is depicting Shaka's greatness with such skill that one is deluded into thinking that his sympathy was with Faku. Technically it is true, for he is implying that his sympathies are with him when he has to meet so dreadful an enemy. In Zulu *mtaka* is used with the feeling of affection.

The characters in Shaka's praise-poem are shown as running away or being completely wiped out by the armies of Shaka. There are unpoetic repetitions which it is clear were not made by the original composer, but by the reciter from whom the author recorded them. The repeated stanzas are not according to any artistic law, but merely are stanzas which the reciter might have forgotten that he has already recited.

The poet never runs short of facts; in fact he has to continually provide space and to avoid crowding his material. He composes with confidence and originality. One never feels that the praise is unjustified because he substantiates his assertions. The poem became an eternal inspiration to the nation and the youth of the country.

Following on this portrait of Magolwana who revolutionized the emergent Zulu poetry during the heroic and consolidating era of Shaka in the early nineteenth century, Mazisi Kunene gave his assessment of another major Zulu poet Mshongweni who recited in the court of King Dingane (1807-1840), one of Shaka's half brothers and assassinator of the Great Zulu King:

There is nothing known about Mshongweni except that he was Dingane's court poet. He was a great poet as the eulogy on Dingane shows. His main contribution to Zulu literature is the highly analytic style. He was a brave poet. He criticized Dingane for his misdeeds without fear of gaining disfavour from him. In so doing he voiced public opinion.

The poet starts off by commenting on the deed that made Dingane win the throne.   Dingane is depicted as tall and dark. He is not like Shaka who fought his own battles. He is in fact a coward:

UNomashikizela uMachiy' impi yakhe.

He is not just a decorated butterfly like most pre-Shakan rulers, but an aggressive type.

The poet points to Dingane's treacherous nature:

Isiziba esinzonzo sinzonzobele,
Siminzisa umuntu ethi uyageza.

He is like a quiet, deep pool that drowns a man who is innocently bathing.

Dingane is not very aggressive for he is:

Imbuzi kaDambuza benoNdlela,
Abayibambe ngandlebe yabekezela,
AyinjengekaMdlaka ngaseNtshobozeni,
Yadabula yaqeda amadoda.

Here a comparison is made between Dingane and Shaka. Dingane, as the poet says, is not as aggressive as Shaka. Dingane is likened to a bitter plant. The fact that he was not aggressive does not necessarily mean that he was docile. He conquered Mgqeheni and Mandeku of the Mlambo clan. The poet makes reference to the fact that he allowed his people to marry when they chose to, contrary to Shaka's policy:

Umalamulela!
Owalamulela abafazi namadoda,
Walamulela izintombi namasoka.

These events, important as they are socially, are not of great national importance.

The element of rejection runs throughout the poem. Dingane is:

Indiha lebabayo njengesibhaha

OR

Uvezi ngimfunene bemzila ngafike ngamudla,
Kanti ngizifaka iloyi esiswini.

The poet states that he had a big and opulent body even during the time of great famine. Times were indeed changing, and changing rapidly, if the plenty that there had been in the previous reign could now be threatened by famine.

Dingane's gigantic size interests the poet; it is physical hugeness rather than heroic greatness.

The heroic greatness of Shaka cannot fade so soon, the Zulus are still a powerful nation. So he says of Dingane, who still holds control over the huge armies:

Ofingqe amehlo wthunzini lentaba,
Ebengangabazingeli bakwaMavela,
Ebebezingela izimbongolwana.

Nevertheless, gone is the security of the old days. Gone is the voice of confidence. The Boers had already sent an emissary to the King asking to be allowed to settle the very 'swallows' of whom Shaka had prophesied. Indeed Dingane was under these circumstances justifiably uneasy:

Indlovu ekulala kuQwambayiya,
Ezinye ziyala ziyathokoza.

He has not paralyzed; however, he still can fight effectively, hence:

Uphondo lweendlovu uMashiqela,
Lushiqela uMadlanga ngasoFasimba,
Inhlabathi yoNdi noKhahlamba,
Ngifice abakwaMalandela beyihlela,
Nami ngafika ngahlala phansi ngahlela.

Note the use of 'lowering' consonants 'ndo', 'ndlo', 'ndla' to express a hard and forced action. Dingane is unfortunate. He is:

Umsuthu owadla izinyosi zemukela,
Abanye bezidla ziyazalela.

In the characteristic Shakan triumphal stanza the poet enumerates the names of all the great people who are related to Mashobana, whom Dingane captured.

Women were not spared, unlike Dingiswayo, who commanded his soldiers to take women back to their homes for, as he said, he did not fight women but men.

The wives and the daughters of Mashobana were captured. There are in stanza   thirty-one characters enumerated in a stretch, whom Dingane is said to have captured and killed. Although the poet tries to vary the stanza by the use of the verb 'za' in the first five verses, and using the verb 'dla' in the rest, the stanza is too long to be without monotony. He has made a cult of enumerating   the names of the victims. It is no more an effective poetic technique combining   form and meaning.

 The poet is not unaware of the beauties of nature. He says of his King:

Umancwaba wezwe lamaphethelo.

This gives special reference to places occupied by Mashobana and Ngwane of Zikodze, King of the Swazis. The swazis, says the poet, were attacked very early in the morning and many prominent national figures were killed.

The poet also refers to the fact that he came back to kill Shaka whilst the armies were going to fight at KwaSoshangane, where they were killed by the poisonous plant---umdlebe:

Inkomo eyabuya yodwa kwaSoshangane,
Obeyaye ngapha wabalekelwa,
Ngokuswela qoqo elimsithayo.

 He does not have the bravery of his brother, Shaka, for he is:

Umalunguza izindonga kande ukuwela.

He is afraid; he does not, like his brother, plunge himself fearlessly into danger trusting his skill in fighting; he carefully examines everything before he commits himself. The poet continues in this strain wavering between praising Dingane and satirizing him. Perhaps in so doing, he is portraying the paradoxical nature of Dingane. Many liked him for the few reforms he had brought about in the country. Many disliked him for the cowardly act of having killed his brothers, thus almost wiping out the House of Senzangakhona. He was also disliked by those who were yearning for the greatness of the days of Shaka. Of these the poet well said:

Ungezwa bethi 'Dlula pheqe kaNdaba baso Vemvanemi,
Emva kwakho bakugodlel' amaklwa nezinqindi.

He further describes how his King, faced with these difficulties, never would tire of sending armies to the North to Mzilikazi and the Swazis. He enumerates the names of prominent Boers who were killed by Dingane. The names of the Boers who were killed by Dingane are coined by the poet to fit into the stanza.

There are names arising from a demand for artistry which are not names of people, but appear to be based on character traits of the person described, e. g. Mabale-ngiphele, uPhambana-nabahluzayo, Hululu-ngesisu-caba.

One thing remarkable about the names enumerated in Dingane's praise-poem is that in most cases Dingane crushes families or people of the same clan rather than a variety of peoples from different tribes. Families or clans enumerated are of the Mashobane's, Khumalos, the Swazis, the Boers, and the Mkhizes. Dingane's conquests were of a revengeful character. Sensing rejection everywhere, a morbid pettiness for eliminating his 'enemies' drives him to murder whole families without any concrete reason in his mind.

Dingane's praise-poem has the vehemence and force of the poetry of the period, e. g.:

> *Umgabedeli onjengebhubesi,*
> *Odonswe ngezintaba ezimakhelekethe;*
> *Injonmjolo eziziba zolwandle,*
> *UVezi, uMabhakamela!*
> *Owabhakamela inkunzi yakwaBulawayo,*
> *Uqamana! UMndabende wamakhanda.*

There are a few passages which could be removed with good effect. On the whole the poem is good, the poet uses beautiful word pictures, e. g.:

> *Umthunduluka waseMpama,*
> *Izimpangele ziyawulababela.*

OR

> *Insimu ethe ukuvuthwa, yaxholoba,*
> *Yakhanga izinyoni; zathi ukusuka,*
> *Zayidla amanhla, zashiya amazansi.*

The structure of the poem, though not as neatly interwoven as that of Shaka's praise-poem, is superior to the pre-Shakan type. It is 'relaxed' without being too simple or prosaic.

The sure and confident voice begins to falter. There is a note of doubt and a lack of trust that now and then appears in his eulogy.

Mshongweni has aptly described the character of Dingane. He accurately draws the picture of the times in the most poetic language. He has a highly forceful style. The tremendous force of his personality manifests itself in his highly impressive verses. He is a poet of the age without being local in attitude. He is original and has the qualities of a great poet.

These four relatively long excerpts from Mazisi Kunene's earliest critical work, *An Analytical Survey of Zulu Poetry: Both Traditional and Modern*, on the genealogy of Zulu poetry over several centuries, on Shaka, on Magolwana and on Mshongweni, undoubtedly indicate the profound identification he had from the beginning for the expressive representations that embody and articulate African cosmological systems.

One reason for these long quotations is to educate myself on the answer to the question I posed to him in a Keynote Address "The Return of Mazisi Kunene to South Africa: The End of an Intellectual Chapter in Our Literary History" nearly twenty years ago in 1993, on the occasion of his retirement from UCLA and imminent departure for home after spending thirty four years in exile. The question I posed to him then while he was sitting in the front row of the auditorium with his family and an audience of about a hundred people was why of all the important African writers of the postcolonial era he was one of the very few who had aligned himself with African Literature in the African Languages in contradistinction to the overwhelming majority who had succumbed to the debilitating colonial tradition of African literature in the European Languages, from Léopold Sédar Senghor (from Senegal) to Tichaya U Tam'si (from Congo/Brazzaville), from Christopher Okigbo (from Nigeria) to

Lenrie Peters (from Gambia), from Ezekiel Mphahlele (from South Africa) to David Rubadiri (from Malawi). I did not have an answer to this question I had posed for myself through Mazisi Kunene. It is clear to me now that because of his immersion in and complete identification with African cosmology and also because of his inexhaustible knowledge of South African writers who wrote in the African languages, from Mshongweni to Benedict Wallet Vilakazi, from Magolwana to S. E. K. Mqhayi, from J. J. R. Jolobe to Emmanuel Anthony Henry Made, he was able to withstand the power and the effect of colonizing European modernity on the question of language. This strong cultural resistance displayed by Mazisi Kunene shows that he believed as strongly as Clement Martyn Doke that the African languages possessed a genius equal to that of other languages in the world. This explains his hostility towards H. I. E. Dhlomo. About thirty years ago when I knew very little about H. I. E. Dhlomo, whenever I asked Mazisi Kunene about him he would steadfastly refuse to respond but always told me about his older brother, R. R. R. Dhlomo who had written several historical novels in the Zulu language about Zulu kings of the nineteenth century. When today I recollect about this, I believe that R. R. R. Dhlomo was one of the sources of Mazisi Kunene's knowledge about African cosmology as well as, perhaps, one of the inspirations for his Shaka epic. In this context I should mention also that about thirty years ago Mazisi Kunene repeatedly mentioned to me that it was a real pity that Wole Soyinka chose to write in the English language rather than in the Yoruba language given the extraordinary richness of Yoruba culture. Today when I reflect on this, I think he was alluding to the fact that because of the strength of African cosmology within Yoruba culture, had Wole Soyinka written in his mother tongue, his writings would have had or would have possessed, greater cognitive power than those he has given to posterity. When Mazisi Kunene said many of these things to me I was between the ages of twenty-five and twenty-seven, when Marxism, Jean-Luc Godard, my girlfriend and my car were more important than political and cultural matters concerning African languages, even though my Marxism was beginning to gravitate to the view that the European languages were imperializing forces in Africa. Perhaps this gravitating was made possible by the writings of Frantz Fanon and Amilcar Cabral which I was then intensively reading.

All of this leads me to conclude that the persistence exemplified by Mazisi Kunene was made indomitable by his belongingness in African cosmological systems.

Is Mazisi Kunene's poetry a celebration of Pan African values?

It would seem to me, as I quoted earlier, when Aimé Cesairé wrote that "This heritage of Kunene, this great spokesman is without a doubt indispensable to the restructuring of the foundation of the reconstruction of the identity of the African continent," it was among other things, a recognition of the Pan African values that resonate in or inform the work of the African poet. The fundamental principle of Pan Africanism is the aspiration for unity of all black people in the world who have been the victims of European domination and oppression. For Cesairé, a man of the African Diaspora, to recognize that Mazisi Kunene has given Africa a sense of identity with which he has empathy and solidarity, is an implicit acknowledgement of this sacred political principle of the black world. One important mission of Cesairé's intellectual and cultural project was his search for the historical significance of Africa in the modern world in order to contribute to the making of African civilization in the twentieth century. His pursuance of this project is made clear in the interview he had with

Rene Depestre in the 1960s in Havana which appears as an Appendix to the 1972 Monthly Review Press edition of *Discourse on Colonialism* (1950): "But I want to emphasize very strongly that---while using as a point of departure the elements that French literature gave me---at the same time I have always strived to create a new language, *one capable of communicating the African heritage.* In other words, for me French was a tool that I wanted to use in developing a new means of expression. I wanted to create an Antillean French, a black French that, while still being French, had a black character" (my italics). There is striking similarity in the words Cesairé uses to praise the genius of Mazisi Kunene and to reflect on his own intellectual project: the preservation of the African heritage while at the same time creatively expanding it towards new historical horizons. Given this, I would say that Pan African values are embodied in the preservation and enhancement of the African heritage which I take to be the other cardinal principle of Pan Africanism on the cultural and literary plane. Let me add that while it was historically imperative for Africans in the African Diaspora to Africanize the European languages because of the destruction of their original languages in the Middle Passage, in Africa there is no historical need to adopt the European languages because the genius of the African languages is still very much exists in their very existence. While Cesairé felt the historical need to 'blacken' the French language, and Langston Hughes sought to impose the poetics of jazz, Negro spirituals and blues on American English, as he stated clearly in his manifesto "The Negro Artist and the Racial Mountain" (1926), there is no historical necessity for such an undertaking in Africa.

There is a poem by Mazisi Kunene which defines not only his understanding and articulation of African heritage but seems, to me, to summarize his conceptualization of African Cosmology, his reflections on the interrelationship between History and Nature, the simultaneity or interpenetration of past, present and future, and the inseparability between the living and the dead. I take the poem "A Note To All Surviving Africans" to be a manifesto summarizing his poetic production over a fifty-year period. Unfortunately, the poem appears only in English translation by the great poet himself in *The Rienner Anthology of African Literature* (edited by Anthonia C. Kalu, 2007):

We erred too, we who abandoned our household gods

And raised theirs with soft skins and iron flesh.

Their priests made signs at our forefathers' grounds

They spoke in a language that was obscure to us.

To win their praise we delivered our children,

But their lips were sealed and without the sacred mark.

Tired of obscurity they invaded our earth,

Plundering the minds of our captured children.

Yet nothing was so foolish as to burn the symbols of our gods.

Then, to follow helplessly the bubblings of their priests

We emulated their ridiculous gestures and earned their laughter.

Now, we dare not celebrate our feast unless purified by fire

Unless our minds are nourished by the Ancestral Song.

We have vowed through the powers of our morning:

We are not the driftwood of distant oceans.

Our kinsmen are a thousand centuries old.

Only a few nations begat a civilization

Not of gold, not of things, but of people.

I do not know of a African poem that represents with such historical depth and conceptual resonance not only the cataclysmic encounter between African history and European history, with the latter imposing on the former the issue of modernity, but also the catastrophic consequences that ensued on the cultural plane. The Pan African values that the poem postulates are based on the singularity that the African people had in common before the shattering and dislocating historical forces of imperialism, colonialism, capitalism and slavery into people of the African Diaspora (New World) and the people of the African continent (Old World). The line, "plundering the minds of our captured children" which divides the poem in two halves and whose central motif is captivity, either in the form of colonialism in the Old World or slavery in the New World, alludes to the difficulties and complications of Africans in the Diaspora in retaining their African languages and those on the continent confronting their incapacity in fostering African cosmological systems. The line "we who abandoned our household gods" reinforces the theme that historical dislocation through the agency of others has been at the centre of the 'African crisis'. Without doing a detailed intertextual analysis, it is possible to contextualize the poem within the philosophic and poetic ideas that have preoccupied the greatest minds of black world in the two preceding centuries: "Our kinsmen are a thousand centuries old" refers not only to the empires of Mali or Songhay or to the various Kingdoms in Africa but specifically to Egyptian civilization as an integral part of African history, and in so doing establishes a lineage of continuity from Fredrick Douglass's great essay of 1854 "The Claims of the Negro, Ethnologically Considered" through Pixley ka Isaka Seme's "The Regeneration of Africa" (1906) to Cheikh Anta Diop's *The African Origin of Civilization: Myth or Reality* (1956); with "Only a few nations begat a civilization /Not of gold, not of things, but of a people" Mazisi Kunene continues his dialogical relationship with Aime Cesaire's *Return To My Native Land* (1938); the three lines "Yet nothing was so foolish as to burn the symbols of our gods./Then, to follow helplessly the bubblings of their priests/We emulated their ridiculous gestures and earned their laughter" not only resonate with the central theme of Okot p'Bitek's Acholi classic *Song of Lawino* (1966) but also endorses Amilcar Cabral's central political theme of 'return to the source' through political transfiguration (*Return to the Source: Selected Speeches*, 1973); the first two lines "We erred too, we who abandoned our household gods/And raised theirs with soft skin and iron flesh" reminds one of Christopher Okigbo's poems of the early 1960s collected in *Labyrinths* (1971). As these examples show, the Pan African dimensions of this poem are extraordinary. Here I refrain from making intertextual references to the poems of the Cuban poet Nicolás Guillén.

But I would like to conclude regarding this poem by juxtapositioning it to Langston Hughes famous poem of 1919 "The Negro Speaks of Rivers," without commenting as to their intertextuality:

I've known rivers . . .

I've known rivers ancient as the world and older than the flow of human blood in human veins.

My soul has grown deep like the rivers.

I bathed in the Euphrates when dawns were young,

I built my hut near the Congo and it lulled me to sleep,

I looked upon the Nile and raised the pyramids above it.

I heard the singing of the Mississippi when

Abe Lincoln went down to New Orleans,

And I've seen its muddy bosom turn all golden in the sunset.

I've known rivers:

Ancient, dusky rivers,

My soul has grown deep like the rivers.

What these two poems by Mazisi Kunene and Langston Hughes unquestionably indicate or postulate is that the Blues Form comes directly from African Cosmology. The similarity or adjacency of Blues and Cosmology across the historical divide of the Atlantic is at the center of the unity of Pan African values.

Following the death of C. L. R. James in May 1989 at the age of 88 years, a few months later, if I remember correctly, it was probably in late September or early October, UCLA organized a memorial in which Mazisi Kunene read this powerful elegy "Tribute to C. L. R. James: A Great African and a Great Freedom Fighter," which subsequently appeared in the first inaugural issue of *Emergence 1* journal (Fall 1989) produced by the Department of Film and Television at the university:

Those who have nourished the earth

Who have planted the dark forest on the mountain

Command our children to celebrate and open the gates

To acclaim the heroes who bore the fruit

And feed all generations with the spider's vision

When we have tasted the spring from the deep ocean

We shall climb the high mountain of stars

To praise the sacred snake in the centre of the sun

Forever and ever our generations come and go

But the Ancestral stool is like the earth

Life is suspended on a round boulder like time

And from us emerges the eternal dream

We are awoken from a violent sleep by the echoes of love

Our clan is blessed with a thousand rivers

Through a vast morning our sound is replayed again and again

Our eyes open to praise him

We have brought him back to our spring garden

To walk proudly until our shadows and his emerge with those of the earth.

The elegy gravitates around the central theme that was a constant of his voluminous work: the unity of Nature and History in a cyclical process in which the former is more determinant than the latter. Here the process is a constant reinvention of the beginning which is already the end without the phenomenological change of status. Even though James was a Marxist, Mazisi Kunene argues that his Africanness (Nature) supersedes his Marxism (History) and hence him being recalled to the Ancestral world of African cosmology where the present and the past are simultaneous with each other, negating the differentiation of spatial and temporal dimensions. Here Mazisi Kunene is implying the spiritual inseparability of Africa and the African Diaspora despite the rupturing effect of European imperial history.

Mazisi Kunene read the elegy with tremendous power and force, presumably reflecting the strong personal friendship between them during his London years, as he was later to inform me. I was in the audience listening to him reciting it since I was partly there because I had been requested to give a short paper on

C. L. R. James's relationship to Africa. James' political understanding of Africa during the decolonizing moment was in many ways incomparable: indeed, his book *Nkrumah and the Ghana Revolution* (1977) is in the same league as Fanon's *The Wretched of the Earth* (1961) and W. E. B. Du Bois' *The World and Africa* (1938) in giving to Africa from the Diaspora the certitude of its Africanness. It would seem to me that this was a seminal contribution to the continent in the twentieth century when its ontology had been shattered. It would seem to me that the elegy celebrates this.

In what ways did the oral literature of the Zulus of Southern Africa play a prominent role in Mazisi Kunene's literary development?

There can be no doubt that Mazisi Kunene had an unmatchable understanding of the genealogical structure of the poetic form of oral literature as indicated by his thesis *An Analytical Survey of Zulu Poetry: Both Traditional and Modern* which was a landmark document on the occasion of its presentation in 1958 or 1959 (it does not show the date of its submission to the University of Natal) and has not been surpassed in the subsequent forty years since its impact on studies of African literature in the African languages beginning with Albert Gérard's *Four African Literatures: Xhosa, Sotho, Zulu, Amharic* (1971). The thesis itself has become a great historical archive in the study of South African cultural forms. In fact, it facilitates a comparative study on a continental scale of African cultural forms. I would like to postulate retrospectively that Mazisi Kunene's thesis is one of the pillars of my New African Movement website. One of the most astonishing things about the thesis is the calm self-assurance with which Mazisi Kunene traverses its complex longitudinal structure and the impression he gives that this is his imaginative and historical territory in which he belongs by virtue of his genius of which he had strong belief. When I first met Mazisi Kunene in 1974 or 1975 in Los Angeles, I was struck by his incredible kindness and great Humanism and his love and belief in Africa. I knew absolutely nothing about him except that I was vaguely aware that he was an author of a book called *Zulu Poems* which I had not read. I must amend this slightly by mentioning that I had read one or two of his essays, one of which was most certainly "Revolutionary Challengers and Cultural Perspectives" which was anthologized in the then recently published *New African Literature and the Arts*, vol. III (1973) edited by Joseph Okpaku. During our first meeting he was 43 or 44 years old and I was 26 years old. I was startled by his conveyance to me through his resolute seriousness and his belief that he was destined for greatness. Of course then I was not aware that he had been a child prodigy writing poetry at the age of 8 or 11 years old and had been actually published in newspapers. I was not aware too then that he had already written several epics which were carelessly scattered around his flat or apartment in London, as Mofolo Bulane mentions in the aforementioned article I quoted earlier. All of this is to say, it is only upon reading his thesis in the 1990s, which was photocopied and sent to me by an Indian librarian at the University of Natal for which I'm grateful, that I became aware of his intellectual seriousness which was based on a deep study of the great poetic tradition of Magolwane and Mshongweni (nineteenth century) and Benedict Wallet Vilakazi (twentieth century), subsequently supplemented by his passionate readings of Geoffrey Chaucer, Pablo Neruda and Aimé Césaire. When he settled to teaching at UCLA (University of California in Los Angeles) in the 1970s, he studied many epics and mythical narratives from different areas of the world: from the *Mahabharata* (India) to the *Popol Vul* (Guatemala), from the *Mwindo Epic* (Congo) to the

Ramayana (India). Auditing his Seminar in the Spring Semester of 1989, on returning to Los Angeles from Europe after an absence of ten years, I was fascinated by his engagements with Amerindian civilizations. That he was familiar with Homeric epics is a given that he had a good South African education before 'Bantu Education' was instituted in the early 1950s. Let me add here that in growing around Durban, he had an appreciation for Indian culture(s). He expressed respect for it to me on several occasions.

If we were to set adjacent to each other two important literary histories of African literature in the African languages to form a triad with Mazisi Kunene's An Analytical Survey of Zulu Poetry: Both Traditional and Modern, A. C. Jordan's *Towards An African Literature* (1973), assemblage of essays written in the 1950s, Benedict Wallet Bambatha Vilakazi's *The Oral and Written Literature in Nguni* (1946), the innovativeness of Kunene's is apparent. Whereas the approaches of Vilakazi and Jordan are diachronic in purpose, that of Kunene is synchronic in effect. That being the case, Kunene was singularly engaged with the metamorphosis and morphology of a poetic form, especially its passage through two historical moments dominated by the aforementioned two great Zulu poets. As a consequence of his approach, Mazisi Kunene was struggling with understanding the *classicism* of the Zulu language. Perhaps Kunene could afford to construct the endogenous form of Zulu literature because his 'master' Vilakazi had already done the much harder task of formulating its exogenous sequencing imbricated as it was in all kinds ideologies and philosophies of history. This interest in the classicism of an African language connected Kunene to the great Xhosa poet S. E. K. Mqhayi who was engaged with purifying the classicism of the Xhosa language which was part of his struggle with his predecessors the Xhosa Intellectuals of the 1880s (William Wellington Gqoba, Gwayi Tymzashe, James Dwane, Pambani Jeremiah Mzimba, Elijah Makiwane, Isaac W.

Wauchope, John Tengo Jabavu, and John Knox Bokwe). At this time of searching for the lineages of the classicism of the Zulu literature, Kunene was virulently hostile towards the Zulu poetry of Vilakazi whom he accused of having compromised the purism and classicism of the Zulu language by importing the poetics of English Romanticism, especially of Shelley, into his poetic project. It is only a decade later when he was in exile in London in the late 1960s that Kunene expressed an unalloyed appreciation Benedict Wallet's poetry in the "Introduction" to *Zulu Poems* which I quoted earlier.

In short, it is the classicism of Zulu oral literature that Mazisi Kunene transposed into modern Zulu poetry that made him the towering poet he became. This will all be evident in the new publications and translations being presently undertaken in South Africa if this was not evident before.

After twenty-plus years of knowing Professor Mazisi Kunene and maintaining a friendship with him that spanned decades, what fond memories do you have of him as a writer, artist, human being, and revolutionary icon whose principles were deeply tied to his theoretical frameworks for African centred writing?

I have already alluded to his profound human decency which stems from his Humanist philosophy. When I first met the great poet, arguably Africa's greatest poet of the twentieth century, as already mentioned, I did not know that he had been a child prodigy and that he had already written several epics all of which had not as yet been published. I think I had read somewhere in an essay by Alex La Guma, our brilliant critical realist writer and an absolutely uncompromising member of the South Africa Communist Party who died in Cuba in 1986 and is buried there, that Mazisi Kunene was busy writing epics in London. Mrs.

Kunene mentioned to me when she passed through Los Angeles within a year of Mazisi Kunene's passing that she had just retrieved all his London writings from 1959 to 1974 that had been left behind when he came to Los Angeles. These writings too, as far as I'm aware, are part of a huge collection of his unpublished writings that form part of the display that has transformed their home in Durban into a Museum of his Writings. The display of these voluminous unpublished writings is splendidly laid out with tremendous care at the house. I do not know of anyone who has seen them who is not impressed by their enormity. As she was showing me the display in 2008, I remember Mrs. Kunene mentioning that she herself was taken aback by how extensively he had written in exile. In all the years I have known him, he always had in his hand a hardback notebook in which he wrote. Mrs. Kunene informed me as we were touring her display of his great achievement that he bought a new empty notebook every few months having filled the previous one. Tragically, some of the notebooks filled with reams and reams of poetry have been lost. One is left to wonder if he had stayed at home and not gone to exile, would he had written as extensively as he did. Personally I do not think so. The extensiveness of his writings is an index of his political and cultural tribulations in *exile*.

As I mentioned in passing earlier, within a short time of Mazisi Kunene's arrival in exile in London, he was given one of the highest positions within the ANC, that of ANC Representative for the whole of Europe and even some parts of Asia. This afforded him an opportunity to travel to many different parts of the world, and much more importantly, it gave him an opportunity to study many cultures. This enabled him to study and develop an appreciation of Asian cultures, especially Japanese culture. In this he was similar to the great Mexican essayist and poet, Octavio Paz who because of his ambassadorial tasks enabled him study Indian culture and civilization that resulted in the magnificent book *In the*

Light of India (1995). Let me mention in passing that Mazisi Kunene loved Latin American countries and cultures, and wholeheartedly supported the Cuban Revolution even though as a progressive African nationalist he was against the Communist ideology. I partly mention Paz here because his book *The Children of the Mire: Modern Poetry from Romanticism to the Avant-garde* (1974), which is the outcome of the Charles Norton Lectures he gave at Harvard University in 1971-1972, had an incalculable effect on me in understanding modernity as a world historical experience. Retrospectively, I think this book, as well as Perry Anderson's *Considerations on Western Marxism* (1976) and Roberto Fernández Retamar's great essay "Caliban: Notes Toward a Discussion of Culture in Our America," which originally appeared in the English language translation in the *Massachusetts Review* of 1973 (and later assembled in *Caliban and Other Essays*, 1989), were instrumental in enabling me construct the New African Movement website. Much more crucially, I think these texts and many other books gave me an intellectual culture that enabled me to have instant rapport with Mazisi Kunene on our very first meeting each other.

The world of Mazisi Kunene in the upper echelons of the ANC in exile was traumatically overturned by decisions of the National Executive Committee (NEC) at the Morogoro Conference in Tanzania in 1968. The Morogoro Conference was necessitated by a series of crises in the South African liberation struggle: the struggle between Marxism and African Nationalism within the organization; the hostility of American imperialism towards the organization in preference for the Pan Africanist Congress (PAC); the momentary defeat of the South African Revolution by the Apartheid forces in the 1960s; and the Sino-Soviet split. As a result of the decisions that were made at the Morogoro Conference, Mazisi Kunene was among those individuals and political tendencies that were demoted; this plunged the great poet into a deep crisis that led to all kinds of unintended consequences. When he arrived in Los Angeles, he was completely devastated and I can say, unequivocally, a broken man *politically* but not *culturally*. Since I had just completed my doctoral examinations and left only with writing the dissertation, I was in position to drive him all over Southern California in order to help him establish himself in Los Angeles. I also drove him several times to UCLA for interviews that eventually enabled him to get a professorship that made it possible for him to establish himself there for the next nineteen years until he returned home in 1993. On receiving this position, the following year after his first arrival, he returned to London in the summer to get married and start his wonderful family. Perhaps because of this, Mazisi Kunene always treated me as his dear younger brother and later as an intellectual colleague. One thing that truly frustrated him over these years was my Marxism, which unknown to me, was one of the things that had desperately made him leave London in search for an academic job in the States. We dearly respected and loved each other dearly.

I would like to quote a complete letter from him in response to my inquiry about his relationship, if any, to Jordan Kush Ngubane, whom I consider to have been one of the great South African journalists and a major intellectual within the New African Movement. Because he was violently anti-Communist, a political maverick, and ended his last years, having died in 1980, as a staunch supporter of Gatscha Buthelezi and Inkatha Freedom Party. Today, he is summarily dismissed by many of our intellectuals, if they have bothered at all to familiarize themselves with his intellectual work. Although I completely disagree with the politics of Jordan Ngubane, he really fascinates me because his intellectual mind is in many ways first rate. Anyway, here is Mazisi Kunene's Letter (April 13th 2000) in response to my queries about Ngubane, including whether Nyembezi was still alive or not, and including whether in his youth he heard about Josiah Mapumulo and A. Ngidi, Zulu intellectuals who preceded his own constellation of the Zulu intellectuals of the 1940s:

First of all to business first C.L.S.Nyembezi is very much alive he had a stroke but he is recovering very well or shall say 'Jazzically' so I was told by reliable sources I intend to visit him myself as soon as I get settled with what I am doing hopefully if he is well I will carry a tape recorder.

As for Maphumulo and Ngidi I remember their names in my youth vaguely as my father was a great reader of his sacred Ilanga Lase Natal. I don't think they ever wrote any book or any big literally work I will search though from Killie Campbell Centre.

Jordan Ngubane is a complicated character, yes I met him many times in fact he used to come to my place very often fortunately or unfortunately I belong to the Kunene family that means simply I am trained in loyalty. He could call me dogmatic for having felt a certain revulsion for him (motivated by my loyalty to the organization [ANC] therefore needing no alternative opinions the fact that he had joined the liberal party and dogmatically anti-communist made me have a deep contempt for him) at the same time I realised that he was a man , an intellectual with deep loyalties towards western directions of intellectualism. He also was so vicious on Luthuli that I felt protective towards Luthuli whose gentleness and political I knew very well. In this case he seemed to be trading on Luthuli's very soul to the white audience in South Africa maybe my violent judgement on him was based on the fact that I knew Luthuli as my father and I knew his gentleness and generosity. It is a pity that you are not writing on Luthuli that will give you an opportunity to judge on the fundamental question of modernism and so called traditionalism this I think will give you an incredible balance in your judgement and also give you insight on Tambo when you start writing about him.

Nevertheless I still think that Ngubane was a man possessed with a disciplined but misguided political opinions by misguided I mean he was over influenced by western intellectuals. Of course there is Chinese intellectualism, African, Indian, Pre-American intellectualism they are all based on the idea of searching for meaning on a universal scale this we must identify first before we make conclusions about whether this or that is fitting for a particular period or era. Thank God we have reached the era of universalism at least within our planet that for me will be a direction towards modernism it must include all trends positively (towards relevant or a relevant doctrine or doctrines towards universalism)

On 'Jazz' I will comment please treat Jazz as a way founded by African Americans towards modernism they were lucky because their religion was stylised in African directions and therefore we can regard them as a first and the most dynamic force towards recreating an alternative to westernism we must also bear in mind that they were lucky also because they were victims of the most vicious attempts to sterilize them and recruit them as appendages of the western doctrines. Their revolt and reaction in language and in spirit and in the preservation of what remain to define them as African became a quality of reinforcement towards enabling them to define themselves as Africans i.e., as children of Africa this has guaranteed them as our ideological leaders in the sphere of change that is why those scholars and writers in Cuba, Brazil, South United States are correct when they stipulate that they are the keepers of the sacred calabbash.

I hope you still have access to my document which I wrote when I was in America on your instigation on this subject.

There are some people who are on the way to being Africans and there are some who have turned away (ideologically) from being African. It seems to me that the strength of civilizations, modernism etc lies in a people to anchor their persepectives on their past i.e. ideologies that define them.

On Dhlomo I think he was an intellectual writer without doubt but never equate him to the Kunene. The problem we have here is that he tended to address the western audience and was forced to talk as if he was apologetic about his tradition. His brother was lucky in this sense that he was writing in his language, this note the attempts by people who were totally exiled from Africa that they began to create languages that were neo Africa or rooted and based on their ideologies of Africa some take a route of using gaja and rastafarians using hash to re experience (if only in fantasy) the great reality of Africans do not look down on them in their attempts to recoup their individualism, Africanism. Likely we are now moving towards an era that is going to celebrate Africa genuinely without the phony attempts of the so-called intellectuals i.e. pseudo westerns. No one can fully celebrate this quality of intellectualism in a foreign context to do so one must anchor totally in the culture and do I dare say, the language from which he comes from.

Finally my verdict on Kunene and Dhlomo is simply it will take a thousands years for Kunene to be born again.

Hope to hear from you soon.

M. Kunene

In the following Letter (April 11th 2000) Mazisi Kunene was responding to my urging him to start writing or complete the Afterword to my monograph which I had written in 1997 and published in 2007 (*The Cultural Modernity of H. I. E. Dhlomo*, Africa World Press). He was very reluctant to write anything on H. I. E. Dhlomo because he felt had betrayed African culture by writing in the English language; secondly, the reluctance stemmed from the fact that he believed the very act of writing on Dhlomo constituted a betrayal on his part of Benedict Wallet Vilakazi, his 'master'. Eventually, he did write it, for which I'm grateful, but by then he begun to be engulfed by a disease which makes the Afterword difficult to read and understand. For the historical record, I insisted on publishing it in my monograph even though in many ways it is largely incomprehensible. I'm very grateful that he actually wrote it. The great poet never recovered from the disease which led to his passing away in 2007. Here is the complete letter:

Dear Brother Ntongela

One must marvel a creation for having created a species called American. Although this species is limited in many ways it has (pending its deep and ancient cultures of China, India, Africa and Pre-America) unless they imitate and learn from these deep and massive civilization of the past they will be in a position to have created or create for themselves and for humanity in general a great civilization.

Note a new civilization I refer to will combine the actual human civilization i.e. social civilization and mental civilization of crisis called technology and sometimes called modernity. I know this is unfair to you before you absorb the great perceptions that I will integrate into the critic of the introduction to your Masterpiece and great research.

You ask me a relevant question: How is Kunene rated in relation to Dhlomo, Vilakazi *et al.*? Well I think the answer is simply and logical none of these writers wrote with a global and universal perspective because they were trapped in their own era and local problems (note that Kunene transcended the politics from which he learned many things relating to the global challenges) First of all I think Vilakazi was great of course could not be greater than kunene Ha! Kunene is a phenomenal as generations hereafter will affirm. Secondly you noticed that the people that come closer to Kunene's estimation wrote in their language that is Mqhayi, R.R. Dhlomo and Vilakazi they had the challenge to enter into the depths of their souls that stretch invatible (sic) to the eras of their past, nobody who neglects the eras of the contributions of ancient times shall ever be great. The reason to me is obvious greatness issues from the womb of the earth the earth is our mother and all our wisdom comes from this connection and relationship. Yes, the others have made an effort to glorify the spectacular exit of the mind to things visual i.e. the romantics and others but because they abandon the direct challenges of the earth they were punished by the earth and remain interesting but unachored and minimal i.e. not universal. I never underestimated your critcisms in fact I am learning a lot from your thesis [The Cultural Modernity of H. I. E. Dhlomo manuscript] here of course I will have my own views on modernism. I think modernism is a good idea as long as it is not glorified as a psychological condition in other words glorified without realising that it is an instrument of control glorified by those who exercise power. This is in relation to circumstances relating to countries and movements such as missionarism, technological advancement as in ideological statement and justification of exercising power over the technological disadvantaged it means my Dear Ntongela that technology is relevant to the challenges imposed on us by the material crisis of our era. In short we are getting more and more exposed to the scarsity and organisations that relate to the need to transform our technologies in relation to the President but we are warned by history that we should never totally abandon that wisdom that mushroomed from our relations stipulated by our earth base.

My friend here is telling me to wrap up this email and I will since people like her will only get angry inside are more dangerous than those people who frequently express their anger in spectacular demonstrations. I will conclude by saying the obvious, namely that the control of language with all its philosophies is so crucial that it always pulls us back to base and in fact you can define the universe and the universal in terms of our anchorage to the earth. Yes, I know you will disagree with me but after a while you will think and rethink and begin the process of admitting that perhaps Kunene had a point or was right (any chance for that happening).

You asked what am I doing here well here is the answer, I am contested cake between the University of Natal and Natal Technikon on the verge of my being moved from Natal Technikon sent its messengers and said thank you we are here to collect Kunene at which point Natal Varsity said No he is ours since then they had continued say it with a bang by providing me with offices but no telephone thanks to the students who made so many telephone calls that the phone was disconnected unless I paid R27000, which I did not have and still not have therefore I am here at Natal Technikon with three offices with a telephone and peace to write my many Masterpieces. Fortunately there are friends here one of them being the one who is typing for me without pay but hoping to be paid eventually and often capable conversing intellectually with me. I wish this lady on you she is great without realising it if only she could stop one habit which I wont mention it since she is typing this note.

I have a great artist here named Andries Botha who is fanatically looking everywhere for funding for me so that I am totally free from any concern or thought about money.

That explains everything she says to wrap up so I will. Thank you for being there for me to talk to.

Best regards

Mazisi Kunene

Although these letters from Mazisi Kunene, among others, show the nature of the brotherly relation between us, there were instances when we were seriously in disagreement with each other. For instance, for two years just preceding his return home in August 1993, we were not on speaking terms with each other because of the conflict between the African National Congress (ANC) and the Inkatha Freedom Party (IFP), a conflict that was leading the country towards a civil war. The catastrophe was averted by the leadership wisdom of Nelson Mandela as well as by the intervention of leading institutions such as the United Nations. But this is a narrative for another occasion.

You describe Mazisi Kunene's poetry as a beacon of light in a completely dark age, with reference to South Africa. Can you elaborate on this point?

I do not think I could have thought and written that with the exception of Mazisi Kunene the historical moment in which he situated was "completely a dark age" when my country has had so many excellent writers and poets, some of whom are truly great, in the post Second World War era! By universal consensus, it was recognized that it was the politics of *apartheid* that constituted the darkness of this complex age. Also the historical period preceding the War characterized by the politics of *segregation* had its distinct complexity regarding the relations between politics and culture or *cultural politics*. Because of the politics of domination, oppression, enslavement, like many other countries that have undergone a similar historical situation, in South Africa it has been difficult to construct the idea of a *national literature* and formulate its possible *literary history*. Excellent books have been written about South African literary history by Ezekiel Mphahlele (*The African Image*, 1962), Stephen Gray (*South African Literature: An Introduction*, 1979), Michael Chapman (*Southern African Literatures*, 1996) and Christopher Heywood (*A History of South African Literature*, 2004), for example, but none of them in the process of studying the historicity of literary form have attempted to formulate the concept of a national literature, let alone its possible unified structure. It is remarkable that no major study has been undertaken of a national literature of a particular African nation in the twentieth century comparable to what happened in Europe in the nineteenth century. For example, Francesco de Sanctis's two volume *History of Italian Literature* which appeared in the late nineteenth century was in fact a spiritual representation of a nation in a process of formation, despite that the third volume on the nineteenth century itself never appeared because of the refusal of the publisher. Only fragmentary studies of Manzoni and Leopardi subsequently appeared.

I think the decisions of Europeans in the thirteenth and fourteenth centuries in rejecting the hegemonic Latin language and writing in their vernacular languages facilitated the making of a national plasticity that in subsequent centuries made the emergence of a national consciousness possible, whereas in our instance the majority of our writers are illegitimately wedded to the hegemonic European languages and have disdain for African languages, with notable exceptions such as F. O. Fagunwa and Mazisi Kunene. I think explains the incredible musicality of European nationalisms and their terrifying cataclysmic clashes whereas our nationalisms are unmusical and dour, which explains the perpetual reversion to tribalism and other unholy things. One has just to look at Luchino Visconti's *Senso* (1954) and *The Leopard* (1963) to note the absolute musicality of European nationalisms. Europeanism is assisted by distinct forms of monolingualism whereas our particular linguistic textures are intractably multilinguistic, which is not necessarily a bad thing. The limitations of an extraordinary effort such as Chapman's *Southern African Literatures* are not necessarily his personally but reflect the crisis of the African historical imagination. This book by implication shows that South African literary space is not so much characterized by "darkness" but rather as unendingly crises ridden. Mazisi Kunene's prodigious work was an attempt to resolve these crises by means of his incomparable genius. Only posterity will know whether Mazisi Kunene succeeded in being the Shakespeare of African literature, not just South African literature, or not!

Of Mazisi Kunene you once stated that what he knows extremely well is to write great poetry and that writing great poetry is also part of the political struggle. Are you saying that poetry and politics are intertwined? If so, how would you contextualize Mazisi Kunene's oeuvre within this discourse?

Even though I do believe that politics and culture (poetry being a part of this) are inseparably intertwined with each other, they are not reducible to each other. If politics becomes a determinant of poetry, what results from this forced interaction is bad poetry. This is because even though they are inseparable from each other, they each possess a distinct logic of autonomy that makes them respond differently to the temporality of history. It is this temporality of form that has to be respected in each of their complex spheres of autonomy. Politics in relation to culture is dangerous because by its very nature it is an instrument that tends to forge relationships according to its own imperializing dictates. If possible, which is extremely difficult to achieve, it is culture that should be made to set the tone for politics concerning their interactivity. There is a poem by Mazisi Kunene, which is in the *Zulu Poems* (1970) anthology, which I read just a few years after meeting him for the first time in the mid 1970s, that *today* makes me better understand the relationship between culture and politics and also why Wordsworth, Rafael Alberti and César Vallejo were my favorite poets before encountering the great poet. In this lyric, "The Power of Creativity", he makes a distinction between the *politics of creativity* (culture) and the *politics of power* (politics):

> The sea echoes in the caves
> Celebrating its conquest into the darkness,
> Exploding from the belly of the earth
> Until the giant bulls are awakened from their sleep.
> They cry till their voices split the moon.
> Blood flows into the blanket of the skies
> Congealing into coils of mist.

Your power struts on the cliffs like a gorilla.

You return having conquered the earth.

I know, because dawn advances,

You will never be conquered by cowards.

You will break their fortress

Releasing the leaf that has long been buried,

Making it quiver on the shore of great waves,

Kindling the lips that have long been silent.

I would venture to say that the first seven lines of the lyric are about the politics of creativity, and the following eight lines are about the politics of power.

I begin with Wordsworth, the English Romantic poet who arguably brought the Enlightenment and modernity into English literary culture. At the moment of his original productivity in his early twenties, he was a supporter of the French Revolution, even in the paradoxical form of supporting the Haitian Revolution against the French Revolution, as it was carried through Napoleonic terror and dictatorship throughout Europe. Unfortunately, our wonderful British teachers in High School in the postcolonial Kenya of the mid 1960s did not teach us to know this Wordsworth, who was more relevant in our then decolonizing context, but Wordsworth the great Celebrator of Nature in such poems as "Tintern Abbey" and "Intimations of Immortality". The fluidity of poetic form in a poem like "Tintern Abbey" concerning the following themes is what made us ex-colonials to passionately fall in love with poetry. For me, personally when I think about it today retrospectively it prepared me for my encounter with Mazisi Kunene: it is about memory as an active process of mind; memory itself is treated as a defence against time, decay, and loss of divining power; it emphasizes restitution, compensation gain rather than loss; it formulates the synaesthetic sense of seeing/hearing; it meditates on the permanence of human consciousness and nature; although it formulates the renewal of hearing, vision and perception, it gives primacy to hearing over sight, and articulates reciprocity between mind and nature; the lyric configures a movement between images of presence and absence which represent parts and whole; some lines alternate images of fullness and emptiness, of gain and loss, as well as those of height and depth; and lastly, other lines meditate on the distinction between the inside and the outside in relation to the self and nature within the context of earliness and lateness.

Like Wordsworth, I think Mazisi Kunene deals also profoundly with the matter of Memory, the living and the dead, the harmony and disharmony between History and Nature within the African cosmological system. Given this, it was really shocking to discover that Mazisi Kunene hated the English Romantics; this hatred, as already mentioned, is expressed most pronouncedly in *An Analytical Survey of Zulu Poetry: Both Traditional and Modern*. I tend to believe that this animosity was more political than aesthetic, given the context of English colonial domination of Africa. But, for me, the path to Mazisi Kunene was through William Wordsworth. For this I owe a great gratitude to my British teachers in Kenya just over fifty years ago. Nevertheless, I think the Wordsworth that should have been introduced to us in the then decolonizing context should not have been limited to the poet who revolutionized poetic form but also the one who was revolutionary in political outlook as this sonnet "To Toussaint L'Overture" undoubtedly makes clear:

TOUSSAINT, the most unhappy of men!

Whether the whistling Rustic tends his plough

Within thy hearing, or thy head be now

Pillowed in some deep dungeon's earless den;

O miserable Chieftain! Where and when

Wilt thou find patience? Yet die not; do thou

Wear rather in thy bonds a cheerful brow:

Though fallen thyself, never to rise again,

Live, and take comfort. Thou has left behind

Powers that will work for thee; air, earth, and skies;

There's not a breathing of the common wind

That will forget thee; thou hast great allies;

Thy friends are exultations, agonies,

And love, and man's unconquerable mind.

Indeed, an "unconquerable mind" is invariably striving for freedom and justice, which is what we were seeking for in a decolonizing context.

The poet who made me aware of form in poetry and, presumably, made me understand poetry, consequently leading me in the direction of Mazisi Kunene, was the Spanish Communist poet Rafael Alberti, a member of the "Generation of 1898" together with Antonio Machado, Miguel de Unamuno, Juan Ramón Jiménez and others. Following the Spanish Civil War of the late 1930s, like many other progressive intellectuals, he was exiled in Mexico by the victorious fascist regime Francisco Franco. I discovered his poetry in the bookshelves of the Los Angeles Central Public Library during my undergraduate days at UCLA. This accidental discovery in similar circumstances is also true of the other poet I will mention in a moment, the Peruvian Communist poet César Vallejo. I discovered their Communism after falling in love with their poetry. What attracted me to Vallejo was his extraordinary Humanism, whose depth I have encountered in philosophers. I have already mentioned the Humanism of Mazisi Kunene. As to why it was in Alberti, in particular, that I came to an awareness of form in poetry, is still mystifying to me today fifty years after the fact. Perhaps it was an element of Humanism in Alberti too. I discovered Vallejo and Alberti at nearly the same time when I spent two years just reading many, many poets, especially from Brazil, Russia and Hungary. All of these occurred about three or four years before meeting Mazisi Kunene for the first time.

The best way for me to pay homage to these great poets is by quoting from each a poem that not only exemplifies their Humanism but also weds together the politics of creativity and the politics of power which I discovered in the aforementioned Mazisi Kunene's "The Power of Creativity".

Here is "Masses" by César Vallejo:

When the battle was over,

and the fighter was dead, a man toward him

and said to him: "Do not die; I love you so!"

But the corpse, it was said!, went on dying.

And two came near, and told him again and again:

"Do not leave us! Courage! Return to life!"

But the corpse, it was sad!, went on dying.

Twenty arrived, a hundred, a thousand, five hundred thousand,

shouting: "So much love, and it can do nothing against death!"

But the corpse, it was sad!, went on dying.

Millions of persons stood around him,

all speaking the same thing: "Stay here, brother!"

But the corpse, it was sad!, went on dying.

Then all the men on the earth

stood around him; the corpse looked at them sadly, deeply moved;

he sat slowly,

put his arm around the first man; started to walk . . .

In this poem of the 1930s from his book, *Human Poems*, published posthumously and titled by his French widow, Vallejo holds in extraordinary equilibrium the politics of creativity and the politics of power. In contrast to the poems in this anthology, which were largely written in France, the poems he wrote approximately fifteen years earlier while still in Peru and which he himself published in *Trilce* (1922) book, he bends and contorts the Spanish language, that is its syntax (it comes through even in English translation), in completely unexpected ways, as perhaps no other poet has done so in the twentieth century with any other language.

On second thought, here is a poem from Trilce, an anthology which really spells out what modernism was really about in the twentieth century. By the way, 1922 is the year in which all kinds of literary masterpieces were published: Joyce's *Ulysses*, Eliot's *The Waste Land*, and the two novels of the seven-volume novel *Remembrance of Things Past* (*Cities of the Plain* and *Sodom and Gomorrah*). All the poems in this anthology are not titled, as was the case with half of the poems in *Human Poems*. In this instance, they are all designated by their Roman numeral numbers. I have chosen "XLV" for its brevity, but more importantly, for its exemplification of how Vallejo was renewing the Spanish language, thereby opening its creativity to new politics:

I unfetter myself from the sea.
When the waters come to me.

Let us always go out. Let us taste
The stupendous song, the song already sung
With the lower lips of desire.
Oh prodigious maidenhood.
A breeze without salt goes by.

In the distance I smell the odor of marrow
Hearing the profound groping, the chase
Of the keys of surf.

And if we should dip our noses this way
In the absurd
We shall cover ourselves with the gold of having nothing,
And we would pollinate
The unborn wing of the night, sister
Of that orphan wing of day
Which trying to be a wing still isn't.

Vallejo was a revolutionary totally committed to the
perpetual transformation of form.

Concerning Rafael Alberti, it is difficult for me to say why it
was him who opened my consciousness to the nature of form in

poetry. After encountering him, poetry became imperative in my life. In a way, when I reflect back on it, it was Alberti who prepared me for Mazisi Kunene. As to why him in particular, I'm totally clueless. I would like to quote this poem, "I Walked One Whole Night With My Eyes Closed" from Alberti's 1929-1930 book of poems, *Sermons and Dwellings*:

The Milky Way was dying to lie down for just one
    hour on the wheat,
one hour to forget so much spilled road,
so many last echoes of heroic, anonymous souls
    retrieve by the wind.
I know now how to escape blindly those towers that will
    question the dawn about the origin of my birth.
I am he,
he who follows the airways of his blood without
wanting to open his eyes.
Some birds are born to risk being smashed against
the nearest stars.

My feet have proved that if there are stones in the
sky they are virtually harmless
there where hands choose to rest in the shadow
    of guitars
and hair still recalls the weeping of willows
when rivers die.
Tomorrow, you will hear me proclaim that there are heights

where the ear hears the trail of a leaf
dead ten centuries and that muffled name
floating in the descent of vanished voices.
I no longer need to prove the Earth is round.

With these quotations from William Wordsworth, César Vallejo and Rafeal Alberti, all I'm saying is that these great poets prepared my consciousness for Mazisi Kunene. In the future I will try to write an essay that focuses on my attempt to understand why it was so!

In my interview with Mazisi Kunene seven years ago he reminded me of the importance of Benedict Wallet Vilakazi to African literature and his own poetry. Do you think he adopted Vilakazi as his alter ego or model for appropriating the fundamentals of Zulu mythology/African centred poetry/poetic forms?

As I have already stated above, there is a direct line of continuity between Benedict Wallet Vilakazi and Mazisi Kunene concerning the fundamental issue that African literature should be written in the African languages by New African intellectuals who are black. This does not mean that they thought that this literature written in the African literature constituted the *totality* of African literature in South Africa. They were very much aware that Afrikaner writers writing in the *Afrikaans language* were like themselves resisting the hegemony of the English language. To extend the logic of this position, though they never had occasion to express themselves in their critical writings on this specificity, they expected that literature written in the *Yiddish language* by the Jews in South Africa was definitely was part of this African literature; likewise a literature written in *Gujerati* and other Indian languages by Indians in my country was also included in this totality; it follows too that the literature by Coloureds in *Afrikaans* was also included; and so on. And of course English literature by English South Africans would also form part of the whole. My understanding of them is that ideally all the languages of South Africa would be represented by literary practices or creativity in the cultural space of South Africaness. One fundamental distinction between them is that Vilakazi as a scholar was principally engaged with the historical poetics of literary systems, whereas Kunene concentrated on their cosmological substratum. This was partly because Kunene preoccupied himself with writing voluminous poetry, whereas with Vilakazi, in comparison with his protégé, one could argue is more important for posterity as a scholar rather as a poet or a novelist. Some scholars would take issue with what I'm saying here.

All this leads me to say that Benedict Wallet Vilakazi was one of the major New African intellectuals of the New African Movement. Probably the best way to know who he really was is by examining the seven literary portraits of him that H. I. E. Dhlomo published in South African newspapers and magazines from about a decade before he passed away in 1947 to nearly another decade thereafter. In other words, Dhlomo was entranced by the intellectual brilliance of his close personal friend. Rather than summarizing all of these intellectual portraits or quoting from all of them, I think it is better for me to quote from the most comprehensive one which appeared in *Drum* magazine ("Dr. Vilakazi", July 1952), a few years before Dhlomo himself passed on:

> Like most mission children, he attended school as a matter of course. In those days education meant almost invariably a teacher's course. So Vilakazi became a teacher, but showed no marked ambition. The change

came later when he was called upon to decide between two teaching posts, one in a comparatively remote and lonely rural post, and the other near a town, with all its attractions.

He chose the rural post. It was the turning point in his life. He began to take keen interest in private studies and received much excellent assistance from the Catholic priests with whom he worked that he became one of the leading African scholars in Latin and preferred to read Virgil and other Latin classics in the original, not in the English translation, which he regarded as inferior. These contacts had profound influence on Vilakazi as artist, scholar and believer . . . In his B. A. course Vilakazi specialised in African Studies. On completing his B. A., he was appointed to the Bantu Studies Department of the University of the Witwatersrand. Thus he became the first African to teach in a European [white] university, a sensational achievement in those days . . . He had three main ambitions. First, to have his times be regarded as the Vilikazi Age in Bantu literature; second, to be one of its leading scholars and greatest men; third, to wrestle from European experts certain academic fields in which he would be recognised as a leading authority. There is no doubt that when he died he was already the most outstanding figure in Bantu literature as original writer, critic and research scholar. Academically, he had outpaced many who had an advantage of many years' start before him. But it is doubtful if the present age will be called his age for time was against him, but in favour of his equally determined rivals. True genius and the highest quality only can defy time, as in the cases of names like Keats, Shelley, Schubert and others. As we began, so let us end. Vilakazi came to be regarded as the cultural Bambatha of his people. He waged great battles for their cultural glory.

I think this literary portrait of his 'master' very closely

resembles that of Mazisi Kunene. Many of us in the 1970s in Los Angeles used to tell him that he was the greatest African poet then alive, when he was despondent that the oppressed people of South Africa had lost so much and had himself moments of doubts whether South Africans really appreciated what he was doing for the Nation despite his bitter struggles within the ANC leadership which he felt had completely defeated him. Now more than ever I'm convinced that Mazisi Kunene was the literary Shaka of African literature for the whole continent. As mentioned earlier in this interview, it was gratifying to know more that a decade later in 1987, when J. M. Coetzee and Andre Brink in their anthology of current South African writing, *A Land Apart: A Contemporary South African Reader*, referred to Mazisi Kunene as a "great poet". Both Brink and Coetzee are among our major writers today. Having become a Nobel Prize for Literature in 2003, J. M. Coetzee is regarded today as a world literary figure. Equally gratifying too was to note thereafter that the most renowned literary scholar in South Africa today, Michael Chapman, in his obituary notice on Mazisi Kunene regarded him equally as a "great poet" ("Obituary", *Current Writing: Text and Reception in Southern Africa*, vol. 18 no. 2, August 2006).

Lastly, I think the profile of Mazisi Kunene is beginning to emerge in a serious manner in the international context. I'm referring to the fact that in Pascale Casanova's highly acclaimed book translated from French, *The World Republic Letters* (1999, 2004) by major contemporary intellectuals such as Perry Anderson, Fredric Jameson and Terry Eagleton, some even comparing it to Edwars Said's *Orientalism*, Mazisi Kunene is mentioned twice in passages that deserve to be quoted in full:

> The work of the South African writer Mazisi Kunene, who has produced English versions of Zulu epics that he himself was the first to transcribe, derives from the same logic. For writers in small nations, internal

translations are an effective way of gathering together available literary resources . . . (p.239). The case of the South African poet Mazisi Kunene (b. 1930) is very similar to that of Boudjedra. As a writer involved in the struggle against Apartheid who served as the representative of the African national Congress to the United Nations in the 1960s, he started out collecting and analysing traditional Zulu poetry [she is alluding to *An Analytical Survey of Zulu Poetry: Both Traditional and Modern* which has been at the centre of my own reflections on him] later creating works of his own in Zulu. Working with poems from the oral tradition, he composed epics that recounted the memory of his people and translated them himself into English, publishing these versions in London, notably *Zulu Poems* (1970) and *The Ancestors and the Sacred Mountain* (1982).

Unquestionably his most important work is *Emperor Shaka The Great* (1979), an epic in seventeen books. His decision to write in Zulu, together with a faithfulness to the forms of oral culture, permitted him to reconcile participation in national politics and the need for international recognition. (p. 239, 268)

Although Mazisi Kunene has not as yet received the international recognition he deserves, I'm totally convinced that it will come in due course when his voluminous manuscripts are published in the Zulu original and through translations, preferably into French, because as *The World Republic of Letters* convincingly argues, it is Paris that has arbitrated international reputations from practically corners of the world in the nineteenth and twentieth centuries. Mazisi Kunene will eventually be recognized as the greatest poet to come from Africa in the twentieth century. With the recognition of his true greatness, his influence on his contemporaries will become even more apparent as a book much a few months ago has startlingly revealed: Roger

Field's *Alex la Guma: A Literary & Political Biography* (2010) indicates quite a few instances in which Mazisi Kunene had a profound impact on Alex la Guma in his early years of exile, though later because of irreconcilable ideological reasons they even stopped talking to each other. For instance, when Alex la Guma passed through Los Angeles in 1977 or 1978 while invited by the American Communist Party, I met him purely by accident at the house of a Party member, and inquired whether he would be interested later in meeting with Mazisi Kunene while he was there, but he gave me a stony silence. When I mentioned this to Mazisi Kunene the following day, he just passed over the matter into other things. So, I'm startled and truly saddened to discover over forty years later that they were at one time very close friends and comrades.

In your appreciation written shortly after Mazisi's passing, you mention that he intimated to you over a thirty year period that his singular mission in life was to destroy African literature in the European languages because he felt it was a "literature of occupation," a deadly cultural poison left behind in Africa by colonialism and imperialism. In evaluating his career, do you think he succeeded in accomplishing this tall order or mission?

What an interesting and difficult question! I'm glad it is the last one in the series of truly challenging questions. No serious scholar of African history and culture can doubt that African literature in the African languages is a direct consequence or product of the violent entrance of European modernity into African history and the imposition of capitalism, imperialism and colonialism on the prevailing pre-colonial social formations and systems of governance. African literature in the European languages, which did not exist in the pre-colonial era, is a direct product of this violent encounter. This is the reason that Mazisi Kunene regarded this literature as a "literature of occupation". Let me quickly add too that *modern* African literature in the African languages in written form is also the result of this violent encounter. Here I'm speaking of the non-Muslim Africa. The critical question here is the issue of *modernity*; this modernity invariably was or is European modernity, colonial modernity or capitalist modernity. One of the fundamental issues in the political and cultural history of South Africa in the twentieth century was the attempt by New African intellectuals to transform European modernity into New African modernity. This was the preoccupation of what is called the New African Movement, a modern awakening whose origins can be traced from the 1860 essays of Tiyo Soga, the first modern New African intellectual, to the collapse of the Sophiatown Renaissance in 1960, defeated by the white supremacist state symbolized by the Sharpeville Massacre of that year. African languages were utilized by some of the New African intellectuals as cultural instruments for transforming European modernity into New African modernity. This occurred simultaneously with the outbreak of a political warfare in the 1930s within the Movement between Marxism and African Nationalism. I have struggled with all of these issues on my New African Movement website (URL: http://pzacad.pitzer.edu/NAM/) for the last fifteen years so I do not wish to say much here. The real question here becomes whether there can be "alternative modernities". Here I follow the position of Fredric Jameson: there can only be a *singular modernity* (Fredric Jameson, *A Singular Modernity: An Essay on the Ontology of the Present*, 2002). This is what Jameson has to say on this contentious and complicated matter in the Introduction: On Not Giving Interviews to *Jameson on Jameson: Conversations on Cultural Marxism* (2007):

As for China and Brazil, the two places in which my work has always aroused the greatest interest (something I have been very gratified by), I'm sorry to say that after the publication of *A Singular Modernity* (2002), in which the very concept of "alternate modernity" was dismissed, my Chinese and Brazilian readers seem to have parted company with me, accusing me of being yet another Western or first world theorist preaching to the rest of the world and seeking to impose Western theories on it. I must still feel, unfortunately, that the only possible "alternate modernity" open to us today is called *socialism*, and that merely *cultural versions of these forms* of difference are not very helpful. But perhaps what pained my critics more was less the attempt to impose my Western thinking on them than my expectation that they would develop alternatives that might reenergize us in the West or the first world: an expectation perhaps too hard to live up to (p. 7, my italics).

At the superstructural level there are a multiplicities of modernisms (cultural expressions, but at the infrastructural level there can only be a singular modernity, at least so far in history).

At the centre of these complex matters is the question of whether the English language culturally speaking can ever become an African language: Mazisi Kunene and Ngugi wa Thiong'o, among others, say NO, but Chinua Achebe and Wole Soyinka, among others, say absolutely YES.

To what extent the publication of the voluminous writings of Mazisi Kunene will change the national situational context of this question in the favor of the African languages only time will tell.

At present there is a growing tragic evidence of a profound crisis regarding the African languages in South Africa, with most of black pre-College students rejecting them in preference for the English language (Thandeka Mapi, "African Languages Are Cool, OK?", *Mail & Guardian*, October 15, 2010).

Lenin at a crucial moment in Russian history asked the question: What is to be done? The answer in South Africa is: a cultural revolution in thinking and a political revolution in implementation.

Printed in the United States
By Bookmasters